Dedicated to Byron Taylor

Copyright © 2019 by Taylor Academics, LLC.
ISBN 9781088726563

Table of Contents

Introduction

The purpose of this book is to provide practice tests and relevant information for passing the hospice and palliative care certification examination. These practice tests follow the five topics covered on the examination: scientific knowledge, professionalism, education and communication, systems issues, and the nursing process. A brief overview of what to expect is dedicated to each topic in *Pearls for Passing* and have been incorporated into the practice tests in a manner similar to the certification exam. Rationales are provided for each of the correct answers.

Opioid conversion problems are typically given in a patient scenario. For this reason, the candidate should know basic opioid conversion as well as the usual opioids used in hospice and palliative care. A chapter is dedicated to this with examples and patient scenarios.

Many of the questions on the certification examination require knowledge of certain scales that are used in the hospice and palliative care arena. These scales are important because Medicare also uses these scales for eligibility requirements and documentation purposes. These scales are supplied in the final chapter of this book.

A vast amount of research has gone into managing end-of-life issues. Although some research must be qualitative due to the issues surrounding death, there has been copious quantitative research that has been proven to improve quality of life. Examples provided in the practice tests include preserving function when a tumor invades the spinal cord, knowing what types of cancer have the highest incidence of pleural effusions, and how to manage bowel obstructions in end-of-life care.

Good luck in becoming credentialed in this noble field.

Chapter 1

Nursing Process: Practice Test 1

The Nursing process section is the largest portion of the test, encompassing approximately 31% of the test. These questions focus on physical and psychological history and assessment, social and family history, evaluation and intervention, pharmacology and non-pharmacological approaches to care, and goals of care. Ready, set, let's begin!

1. The term "refractory" or "intractable" when talking about symptoms means:

    A) Symptoms that require more aggressive treatment.

    B) Multiple approaches have been used to manage symptoms and have failed.

    C) Symptoms that occur as a side effect of aggressive therapy.

    D) Symptoms that have subsided due to medical intervention.

2. The need to increase opioids at certain times in cancer patients is primarily due to:

    A) Cancer progression.

    B) Opioid tolerance.

    C) Opioid addiction.

    D) Opioid non-compliance.

3. Palliative sedation:

    A) is used to relieve refractory symptoms such as dyspnea, agitation, and pain in the imminently dying.

    B) is the use of aggressive opioid therapy to induce a state of sedation for the management of uncontrolled pain.

    C) is only used during inpatient acute episodes of uncontrolled symptoms.

D) does not require a DNR order or written consent.

4. Which exam would NOT be performed on a patient with neutropenia?

A) Central line insertion.

B) PET scan.

C) Rectal exam.

D) Blood draws.

5. What is important to check prior to prescribing medication for a patient?

A) The patient's vital signs.

B) The patient's name and address.

C) The patient's drug allergies.

D) The patient's age.

6. A patient with ALS is decompensating and has an oxygen saturation of 84% on 6L of oxygen via nasal cannula. The family calls you, extremely upset, and wants to know what you can do. You should first:

A) Give an opioid to help with symptoms of dyspnea.

B) Tell the family to immediately call 911, and have the patient transferred to the hospital.

C) Tell the family it is an expected part of the disease process.

D) Assess the goals of care and advance directives.

7. All of the following are examples of non-pharmacological interventions for managing dyspnea EXCEPT:

A) Pursed lip breathing and diaphragmatic breathing.

B) Sitting in a chair, with arms resting on legs, and leaning slightly forward.

C) Elevating the head of the bed.

D) Laying supine with feet elevated.

8. Which statement from a patient requires immediate intervention?

A) "When I was first diagnosed with cancer, I thought about killing myself, but now I don't think about it as much."

B) "I wish I were dead."

C) "I'm okay with dying. I have made my peace, and I'm ready to go. I have my will and finances in order and have saved up enough pills to end my life."

D) "I won't let this disease kill me. I will kill myself before it does."

9. On the Functional Assessment Screening Tool (FAST), at what stage is a patient classified as *'ambulatory ability is lost'* or *'cannot walk without assistance.'*

A) 7E

B) 6C

C) 6B

D) 7C

10. Which patient with CHF is eligible for hospice?

A) A patient with dyspnea with most activity, and an EF of 20%.

B) A patient with frequent angina, is resistant to standard nitrate therapy, and has an EF of 30%.

C) A patient with a NYHA Class III CHF, history of syncope, and HIV.

D) A patient with dyspnea at rest, NYHA Class IV CHF, and is unable to carry out minimal physical activity without angina.

11. Which example best describes physician-assisted suicide?

A) The physician administering an IV push of potassium into a patient's IV line.

B) A physician prescribing excessive amounts of benzodiazepines and explaining to the patient how to take them so they can end their life.

C) A physician prescribing conscious sedation for a patient that is nearing death.

D) A physician giving excessive opioids to control pain in a dying patient, which may hasten their death.

12. On the Palliative Performance Scale (PPS), patients with cancer must have a score of 70% or less to meet hospice eligibility. What score is required for non-cancer patients?

A) 40% or less.

B) 50% or less.

C) 20% or less.

D) 30% or less.

13. Patients with a diagnosis of stroke must have a PPS score of 40% or below to be eligible for hospice. This score indicates the patient:

A) Is mainly in bed for most of the day, is unable to do any activity, needs assistance with all self-care, and has normal or reduced food and drink intake.

B) Has reduced ambulation, limited activity, inability to do housework, occasionally needs assistance with self-care, and has normal or reduced food and drink intake.

C) Patient is totally bedbound, is unable to do any activity, requires total care with ADLs, and can only take minimal sips.

D) Patient is fully ambulatory, but unable to do normal or baseline activities that they were previously able to perform. They remain independent with self-care and have normal or reduced food and drink intake.

14. A 76 y/o female, with metastatic breast cancer, has had a sudden change in her mental status. She starts yelling out at family members and grabbing at the air stating she is seeing things. Her family is very concerned and frightened, because she is typically very alert and oriented to her surroundings. She has been on opioids for many years, but her labs have recently shown a decrease in her renal function. Her family is pushing you to order a CT scan of her brain. You should:

A) Do a focused history and physical relating to her current change in condition, realizing that the patient's delirium is most likely due to opioid-induced neurotoxicity (OIN).

B) Order a CT scan of the brain at the family's request.

C) Order donepezil, since this is most likely the start of dementia.

D) Order Keppra, since benzodiazepines are first-line treatment for delirium.

15. A patient with dementia is said to have the inability to maintain sufficient fluid and calorie intake in the past 6 months when evidenced by a:

A) 15% weight loss or albumin <1.5gm/dl.

B) 30% weight loss or albumin <0.5gm/dl.

C) 20% weight loss or albumin <3.5gm/dl.

D) 10% weight loss or albumin <2.5gm/dl.

16. A 32 y/o female has been on opioids for over two years for ovarian cancer. Her family has noticed that the patient's hand twitches periodically, and they want to know what this is from. You reply:

A) "I will start Keppra since she is having a seizure."

B) "This is called myoclonus and is a side effect from her opioids. I will order clonazepam, which should help."

C) "I will review her labs, but she will most likely have to have an EEG."

D) "This is a sign of dementia and although it doesn't cause any problems, I will start her on an anti-psychotic."

17. All statements are true regarding a Left Ventricular Assist Device (LVAD) EXCEPT:

A) A LVAD is a type of pacemaker with leads entering the left ventricle and atrium of the heart.

B) A LVAD is used in patients with end-stage heart failure and is not the same as a pacemaker because it assumes the function of the left ventricle, instead of only regulating electrical activity of the heart.

C) Many patients have a LVAD implanted as they await heart transplantation.

D) A 2015 study showed 65% of patients died within three years of receiving a LVAD.

18. What indication meets hospice criteria for COPD?

A) Dyspnea with mild exertion.

B) FEV1 of < 30% of predicted after treatment with a bronchodilator.

C) Limited response to bronchodilators.

D) Resting PCO2 >55.

19. A 49 y/o patient with metastatic ovarian cancer is being evaluated for hospice care. What indicator is most indicative of hospice appropriateness?

A) A new liver lesion.

B) A KPS score of 20.

C) A frequency in falls.

D) Frequent opioid increases.

20. A 56 y/o female with pancreatic cancer states she is having severe abdominal pain and nausea. Upon exam, her stomach is distended, high-pitched bowel sounds are heard, and

palpation of her stomach reveals tightness and a moderate amount of gas. She states she has not had a bowel movement in several days. You suspect:

A) Duodenal obstruction.

B) Gallstones.

C) Stool impaction.

D) Diverticulitis.

21. Which indication is most indicative of hospice eligibility in patients with dementia?

A) Decline in labs.

B) Decline in function.

C) Decline in cognition.

D) Increase in hospitalizations.

22. ALS patients can sometimes lose their ability to control their emotions, such as inappropriate laughter or crying. This condition is called:

A) Pseudobulbar Affect (PBA).

B) Emotional Lability Disorder (ELD).

C) Frontal Brain Disorder (FBD).

D) Frontal Cognitive Disorder (FCD).

23. You are evaluating a 72 y/o male with CHF for hospice eligibility. You know he must have NYHA Class IV heart failure to be eligible, which means:

A) Marked limitation of physical activity and is only comfortable at rest.

B) Unable to carry out any physical activity without discomfort, and has dyspnea at rest.

C) Comfortable at rest, but ordinary physical activity results in fatigue, rapid/irregular heart rate, and dyspnea.

D) Patient is oxygen dependent.

24. A patient with end-stage liver disease who continues to drink alcohol:

A) Is most likely a good candidate for hospice.

B) Cannot remain on hospice due to Medicare regulations and guidelines.

C) Should be set-up for an intervention and placed in inpatient care for withdrawal precautions.

D) Should be given a lecture on why they should stop drinking.

25. While you are evaluating a patient, they turn to you and say, "All I want to do is die." You should:

A) Empathize and say I don't blame you.

B) Refer the patient for a psychological evaluation.

C) Tell the patient that physician-assisted suicide is an option.

D) Further explore the patient's feelings and ask why they feel like dying.

26. Patients with PTSD often use what maladaptive coping mechanism:

A) Reflection on previous loss.

B) Excessive use of alcohol.

C) Violent outbursts.

D) Prayer.

27. You walk into a patient's home that has a paid 24-hour caregiver and see that the patient is aspirating on their tube feeding. What do you do?

A) Stop the tube feeding and call the family informing them not to continue it.

B) Continue to let the tube feeding run and update the family on the situation.

C) Have the patient transferred to the hospital.

D) Slow down the tube feeding and inform the caregiver to recheck the patient in a few hours after you leave.

28. Coping mechanisms for loss include all of the following EXCEPT:

A) Online blogging and "chatting" regarding the loss.

B) Distraction therapy such as knitting or playing computer games.

C) Attending support groups and buying a new pet.

D) Remaining on antidepressants, anti-anxiety medications, and prescription sleep medication for over 6 months, because they still "cannot bear to think about it" without crying or becoming unable to function in public.

29. When is it appropriate to NOT honor a patient's wishes, when the patient has been found to be capable of making their own decisions?

A) When the interdisciplinary team's choices are better than the patient's choices.

B) When the patient continually changes their mind and a concrete plan needs to be determined.

C) When the patient's decisions are unsafe, and they are putting themselves at risk.

D) When the patient is making choices based on how much it will cost, instead of what is best for them.

30. Which opioids are typically given to patients with end-stage renal failure?

A) Methadone and Fentanyl.

B) Morphine and Codeine.

C) MS Contin and Hydromorphone.

D) Buprenorphine and OxyContin.

31. A previously active 72 y/o patient with a recent CVA is in a SNF receiving rehab. The therapist approaches you and states that the patient refuses to participate in her therapies and typically stays in her room all day with the blinds closed, sleeping. The therapist is frustrated with the patient and feels she is just lazy. You decide to evaluate her for:

A) Depression.

B) Fatigue.

C) Cognitive impairment.

D) Insomnia.

32. A 87 y/o female who is typically A&O x2 has recently become confused and incontinent of urine. The first test you should order is a:

A) CT scan of the head to r/o stroke.

B) U/A, C&S to r/o UTI.

C) BUN & creatinine to r/o dehydration.

D) CBC to r/o anemia.

33. A cognitively impaired patient is moaning, rocking, and grimacing. You suspect the patient is experiencing:

A) Pain.

B) Anxiety.

C) Sadness and depression.

D) Typical behavior in cognitively impaired patients.

34. Which tool is used for pain assessment in patients with advanced dementia?

A) Pain Assessment in Advanced Dementia (PAINAD).

B) FACES Scale.

C) Universal Pain Assessment Tool.

D) Chronic Illness Pain Scale.

35. It is recommended that patients with an Automatic Implanted Cardioverter Defibrillator (AICD) on hospice care have their device:

A) Removed.

B) Deactivated.

C) Stay activated for quality of life issues.

D) Stay activated and apply a magnet if it discharges a shock.

36. A patient's wife calls you stating her husband has been screaming all night in pain. She says everything she has done for him hasn't worked. She states she is exhausted and doesn't know how much more of this she can take. You suggest:

A) Transferring the patient for inpatient care.

B) Transferring the patient to a nursing home.

C) Hiring a caregiver for additional support.

D) Continuous home care.

37. Which non-pharmacological approach has been shown to be effective for chronic pain?

A) Mindfulness-Based Stress Reduction (MBSR).

B) Meaning-Centered Psychotherapy (MCPT).

C) Psychodynamic Psychotherapy (PDPT).

D) Dignity Therapy (DT).

38. An EKG should be obtained prior to starting methadone on patients with risk factors that include:

A) Renal impairment.

B) Cognitive disorders.

C) A history of substance abuse.

D) Prior EKG with QTc >450.

39. A patient recently diagnosed with lung cancer calls you stating they have run out of their medication early. The patient is on morphine IR 10mg every 4 hours as needed for pain. Your next step is to:

A) Obtain a urine drug screen and switch their morphine to MS Contin 30mg every 12 hours, with morphine IR 5mg every 4 as needed.

B) Inform the patient that you cannot refill their medication early, and they will have to go without.

C) Tell the patient that you can no longer care for them since they are abusing their opioid prescription.

D) Assume the patient is in pain and refill their current prescription early.

40. Which medications are typically used for palliative sedation?

A) Opioids.

B) Midazolam and lorazepam.

C) Anticholinergics and benzodiazepines.

D) Amphetamines.

Pearls for Passing

- Always do **your own** assessment of the patient FIRST, especially before prescribing medication or making a decision regarding care.

- Never take second-hand information as fact from family members.

- Always remember that each patient has their own goals of care. These goals are formed by meetings with the family, patient, and the interdisciplinary team.

- When completing the social history on a patient, it is important to know about the patient's home environment. For example, if a patient lives in a shelter or in a place where their medications have a high likelihood of being stolen, this will affect what you give the patient for pain. Some medications are much less likely to be stolen than others.

- Remember, the most common goal of care in hospice patients is comfort and quality of life. Keep the workup simple and cost effective whenever possible.

- Use evidence-based practice whenever possible with measurable scales.

- There are many different scales used in hospice and palliative care. Know which scale to use and when.

- Know what cancer has the highest association with depression: pancreatic cancer.

- Know how to determine if a patient has decision-making capacity.

- Know what a therapeutic presence is and when it is appropriate.

- Make short-term goals attainable for the patient so that they feel a sense of accomplishment.

- When creating goals for a patient's plan of care, keep the goals realistic and attainable, but never take away hope or the person's beliefs.
- Know how to recognize when a patient is imminently dying, also called transitioning, such as not wanting to eat, sleeping more, and talking about seeing dead relatives. Family members will approach you with concerns; be ready to provide them with education about the imminently dying process, its phases, and what to expect.

Practice Test 1: Answers and Rationales

1. B) Multiple approaches have been used to manage symptoms and have failed.

Feedback: Refractory or intractable symptoms are those that cannot be managed, even with aggressive treatment. Pain and dyspnea are common symptoms seen in hospice patients that can become intractable, and often require transferring the patient to an inpatient hospice facility.

2. A) Cancer progression.

Feedback: Pain management in cancer patients is an important goal of care. Pain presents differently depending on the type of cancer. Usually, as the disease progresses, the pain increases, requiring more opioid management, as well as rotations to different opioids. Tumors can compress or stretch various organs, invade bone, or press on nerves. All of these require a different approach for pain management and should be investigated if the patient has a diagnosis of cancer.

3. A) Is used to relieve refractory symptoms such as dyspnea, agitation, and pain in the imminently dying.

Feedback: Palliative sedation typically does not use opioids. Benzodiazepines, barbiturates, and mild general anesthesia are typically used for palliative sedation. Palliative sedation is only used in patients who are imminently dying, have a signed consent by their healthcare surrogate, and have a DNR.

4. C) Rectal exam

Feedback: Due to the risk of translocation of bacteria into the bloodstream, rectal exams are contraindicated in neutropenic patients.

5. C) The patient's drug allergies.

Feedback: Drug allergies are of major importance prior to prescribing a medication. Most electronic medical records will send an alert, but clinicians should not rely on this. Make a habit of checking the patient's medication allergies prior to prescribing a medication.

6. D) Assess the goals of care and advance directives.

Feedback: You must always first review the goals of care for each patient prior to making decisions, because the plan of care is individualized according to their wishes. Some patients do not want to die in their home and prefer to be transferred to an inpatient unit, while others want more aggressive intervention such as bipap or a high-flow nasal cannula. These other choices may not be in line with the patient's goals of care.

7. D) Laying supine with feet elevated.

Feedback: Orthopnea is shortness of breath while laying supine and can be caused by several factors such as COPD or heart failure. When laying in a supine position there is more fluid absorption, resulting in greater venous return, which leads to increased pulmonary congestion and edema.

8. C) "I'm okay with dying. I have made my peace, and I'm ready to go. I have my will and finances in order and have saved up enough pills to end my life."

Feedback: Studies have shown that 70% of people tell someone they intend to commit suicide, although very few people tell their healthcare provider. When a patient mentions anything about taking their own life, it is important to further address the topic in order to fully assess their actual intent and need for intervention. It is especially important for the healthcare provider to ask about the patient's plan. Explicit warning signs include a well thought out plan, and often include making a will, getting their affairs in order, suddenly writing letters to loved ones, and a sudden change in mood. At this point, the person has most likely devised a means of ending their life. This person should not be left alone, and the provider should call a social worker to help with assessment and intervention.

9. D) 7C

Feedback: A patient must be at stage 7C on the FAST scale to meet hospice eligibility for the diagnosis of dementia. Stage 7C is when the patient loses the ability to ambulate independently.

10. D) A patient with dyspnea at rest, NYHA Class IV CHF, and is unable to carry out minimal physical activity without angina.

Feedback: Patients with CHF must be in NYHA Class IV with significant symptoms at rest. They must be unable to carry out even minimal physical activity without symptoms of dyspnea or angina even though they have been optimally treated with medication. Another indicator for hospice eligibility is angina at rest, resistant to nitrate therapy, and have declined invasive procedures. The patient's EF must be less than or equal to 20%.

11. B) A physician prescribing excessive amounts of benzodiazepines and explaining to the patient how to take them so they can end their life.

Feedback: Physician-assisted suicide is implemented by the physician providing a patient with a means to end their life. The physician is not directly killing the patient but is giving them the means to do so. This is different from ordering conscious sedation for refractory pain in an actively dying patient. Double Effect is a term used when an intervention causes both a positive and negative effect, with the positive effect outweighing the negative. An example is a pain medication given to an actively dying patient, although it may hasten the patient's death. This is not an example of physician-assisted suicide.

12. B) 50% or less

Feedback: Patients without cancer must have a score of 50% or below on the PPS for hospice eligibility, which indicates they mainly sit or are lying down for most of the day, are unable to work, and need considerable assistance with self-care.

13. A) Is mainly in bed for most of the day, is unable to do any activity, needs assistance with all self-care, and has normal or reduced food and drink intake.

Feedback: Patients with a diagnosis of stroke must have a PPS score of 40% or below to be eligible for hospice. This score indicates the patient is mainly in bed for most of the day, is unable to do any activity, needs assistance with all self-care, and has normal or reduced food and drink intake.

14. A) Do a focused history and physical relating to her current change in condition, realizing that the patient's delirium is most likely due to opioid-induced neurotoxicity (OIN).

Feedback: A potential side effect of opioids is opioid-induced neurotoxicity (OIN) caused by the accumulation of metabolites. Patients with poor renal function are especially at risk. Antipsychotics such as haloperidol are typically given, along with hydration and opioid reduction. Studies have shown benzodiazepines have no effect on hallucinations and intensify confusion in patients experiencing delirium. Before ordering expensive tests for the family's sake, it is wise to first do a focused history and physical on the patient to justify a need.

15. D) 10% weight loss or albumin <2.5 gm/dl

Feedback: Dementia patients must be at stage 7C on the FAST scale and have at least one other indicator for decline such as a 10% weight loss, or albumin <2.5 gm/dl in the past 6 months.

16. B) "This is called myoclonus and is a side effect from her opioids. I will order clonazepam, which should help."

Feedback: Myoclonus is a side effect of opioid use and caused by metabolite accumulation evidenced by involuntary twitching of muscle groups. Benzodiazepines are first-line drugs given for this condition. Lab review for hydration status and renal function should be considered. Although this looks like seizure activity, pathologically it is a result from the accumulation of metabolites from opioids; therefore, anti-seizure medications are not considered first-line drugs for this condition. Obtaining labs and completing an exam should be done prior to initiating drug therapy.

17. A) A LVAD is a type of pacemaker with leads entering the left ventricle and atrium of the heart.

Feedback: A left ventricular assist device (LVAD) is not a pacemaker but is a mechanical device that assumes the function of the heart in patients with end-stage heart failure. It is implanted in the patient with a lead that exits the body and is attached to an external battery source. A 2015 study showed a mortality rate of 65% of patients within 3 years of implantation, and an 82% mortality rate within 4 years of implantation.

18. B) FEV1 of < 30% of predicted after treatment with a bronchodilator.

Feedback: As per the GOLD report, stage 4 COPD is reflective of severe lung damage with lung function less than 30 percent of normal. Other indicators for hospice eligibility are PCO_2 >50, dyspnea at rest, and having no response to bronchodilators.

19. B) A KPS score of 20.

Feedback: A score of 20 on the Karnofsky Performance Scale (KPS) means the patient is sick enough to be admitted to the hospital. A score of 50 percent or less is said to predict a median life expectancy of 2 months. A single new liver lesion does not ensure a prognosis of less than 6 months. Increasing opioid doses and frequent falls is not indicative of a 6-month prognosis either.

20. A) Duodenal obstruction

Feedback: Gastric outlet obstruction, secondary to duodenal invasion from progression of malignancy, is a late manifestation of pancreatic carcinoma. Self-expanding metal stents for duodenal obstruction in advanced cancer is often performed. The other answers are incorrect because the obstruction is due to tumor invasion, not stool impaction. Diverticulitis typically presents differently with lower left quadrant abdominal pain. An obstruction should be one of the first things that should be ruled out knowing this patient's history of advanced pancreatic cancer and clinical presentation.

21. B) Decline in function.

Feedback: For patients with dementia, functional decline as reflected on the FAST scale is the most significant indicator for hospice eligibility. The patient *must be at stage 7C on the FAST scale,* as well as having one other indication such as aspiration pneumonia, multiple pressure ulcers, septicemia, or albumin <2.5.

22. A) Pseudobulbar Affect (PBA)

Feedback: Pseudobulbar Affect (PBA) is seen in ALS patients, and is a neurological condition in which the patient is unable to control their emotional responses. An example is when a patient starts crying or laughing for no reason, and then cannot stop.

23. B) Unable to carry out any physical activity without discomfort and has dyspnea at rest.

Feedback: The key terminology for hospice eligibility for CHF is "dyspnea at rest," which places them in classification IV of the New York Heart Association category for heart failure. All of the other answers do not reflect dyspnea at rest. A patient on 2L of oxygen can be resting comfortably without signs of dyspnea, therefore simply being on oxygen does not make them eligible for hospice.

24. A) Is most likely a good hospice candidate.

Feedback: Alcoholism is a disease that has psychological and physiological effects; therefore, the patient becomes physically dependent. Those that have extremely long histories of alcohol dependence, and have end-stage liver disease, need more than just "a lecture." Unfortunately, with end-stage liver disease and the co-morbidities that accompany it, the damage is irreversible and liver transplant is the only option. If the patient still consumes alcohol, this makes them extremely appropriate for hospice care.

25. D) Further explore the patient's feelings and ask why they feel like dying.

Feedback: When patients make statements such as this, it is always a good idea to take the time to further explore why they are making such statements. Sometimes uncontrolled pain or fatigue is the reason, and quality of life can be improved through medically managing these specific issues. Making a quick referral to psychiatry before further exploring the issue can be counterproductive and prolonging treatment for something you could manage.

26. B) Excessive use of alcohol.

Feedback: PTSD and alcohol use are often intertwined. The VA stated up to 80% of Vietnam veterans seeking PTSD treatment have alcohol use problems. This is a maladaptive coping mechanism and needs intervention. Patients over the age of 65 with PTSD, and using maladaptive coping mechanisms such as alcohol use, have a much higher risk for depression and suicide.

27. A) Stop the tube feeding and call the family informing them not to continue it.

Feedback: There comes a time when tube feeding does more harm than good. Stopping the tube feeding and educating the family is an appropriate step in addressing quality of life issues. Goals of care for hospice patients typically addresses comfort and quality of life. Transferring hospice patients back and forth to the ER for life-sustaining measures or aggressive medical therapy would not be in line with typical hospice goals of care. If a patient changes their mind and would like aggressive therapy or life sustaining support, such as mechanical ventilation, the patient would have to revoke their hospice benefit.

28. D) Remaining on antidepressants, antianxiety medications, and sleep medications for over 6 months, because they still "cannot bear to think about it" without crying or becoming unable to function in public.

Feedback: Although bereavement is paid for up to a year by the hospice benefit, it is still considered abnormal if a person does not leave their home or go out in public after two weeks of the occurrence of the loss. That does not mean that the person has completed their grieving process by any means but does raise concerns for the individual experiencing the loss, and their ability to engage in the stages associated with the grieving process.

29. C) The patient's decisions are unsafe, and they are putting themselves at risk.

Feedback: The interdisciplinary team uses the patient's desires and preferences as the basis for their plan of care, unless the patient is putting themselves in harm's way. State and federal law must be acknowledged in developing an appropriate plan of care for a patient. For example, a patient would like to stay in their home and does not want to be placed in a long-term care facility. The patient lives alone and needs around-the-clock care. The patient was found by the CNA lying in their own feces for days and had not eaten. The patient cannot pay for a private caregiver and has no one to care for them. In this situation, it is highly unlikely that this patient's autonomy in making healthcare decisions will be adhered to, primarily due to the safety of the patient and need for social work intervention.

30. A) Methadone and Fentanyl

Feedback: Methadone's metabolites have been found to be *inactive* and are excreted via the gut. Fentanyl metabolites are *inactive* and considered safe to use in renal impairment. Morphine and codeine have *active* metabolites that can accumulate in the presence of renal failure. OxyContin is a trade name for oxycodone, which is synthesized in structure to morphine. MS Contin is long-acting morphine. Hydromorphone, also known as Dilaudid, is a derivative of morphine.

31. A) Depression.

Feedback: Social isolation, and inability to get out of bed and engage in activities, is a clinical sign of depression and should be addressed. The PHQ-9, Patient Health Questionnaire, is one of the most widely used screening tools for depression. A previously active individual, with a sudden loss of function or autonomy, is at risk for depression and is more likely a cause for her behavior than insomnia or cognitive impairment. Fatigue can be a symptom of depression.

32. B) U/A, C&S to r/o UTI.

Feedback: It is very common for the elderly to have increased confusion and urinary incontinence in the presence of a UTI. This should be ruled out first by a physical exam and a U/A, C&S. Order the least expensive tests first to establish a diagnosis. If the patient is not showing signs of a CVA on exam, it is best practice to look for other indications for her symptoms before ordering a CT of the head. Her clinical presentation does not correlate with anemia.

33. A) Pain.

Feedback: Signs of pain in the cognitively impaired is demonstrated by facial expressions such as frowning or grimacing, vocalizations such as moaning, body movements such as guarding or rocking, changes in interpersonal interactions such as resisting care, becoming aggressive or withdrawn, and changes in activity patterns such as appetite or sleep changes. The combination of symptoms is more suggestive of pain, than depression or anxiety.

34. A) Pain Assessment in Advanced Dementia (PAINAD).

Feedback: The PAINAD Scale is used in advanced dementia by rating breathing, negative vocalization, facial expression, body language, and consolability. The other scales are not appropriate for patients with advanced dementia because the patient cannot participate in this type of assessment.

35. B) Deactivated.

Feedback: Deactivation of AICDs is recommended due to cardiac arrhythmias in dying patients and prevents the patient from sustaining painful shocks at the end of life. AICDs at the end of life are shown to decrease quality of life. Deactivation is done by a medical professional, and magnets do not replace the preferred method of deactivation. Surgical removal is not necessary for deactivation.

36. A) Transferring the patient for inpatient care.

Feedback: General inpatient care is appropriate for this patient because it will provide symptom management in controlling his pain, as well as providing a respite for his wife. Continuous home care is very short term, and this patient's care would be better assessed and controlled in an environment that can provide more options for pain control. Respite can be provided up to 5 days with the hospice benefit. This will give his wife time alone in her home and the ability to care for her own needs. Hiring a paid caregiver may not be feasible, and she should utilize the respite benefit covered under Medicare. Transferring a patient to a nursing home is not necessary and can be extremely costly.

37. A) Mindfulness-Based Stress Reduction (MBSR).

Feedback: MBSR uses meditation techniques to help cope with illness, pain, and stress. It focuses on the present moment and is non-judgmental, so the mind can overcome negative thoughts and feelings. Dignity Therapy is designed to assist patients with finding meaning in their lives by writing a legacy of their accomplishments that gave their life meaning. PDPT is a type of therapy that focuses on relieving depressive symptoms by uncovering unconscious thoughts that can contribute to a person's stress and anxiety. MCPT is a type of therapy that addresses spiritual well-being.

38. D) Prior EKG with QTc >450.

Feedback: Risk factors for starting methadone include electrolyte abnormalities, structural heart disease, impaired liver function, endocarditis, a history of ventricular arrhythmia, and a prior EKG with QTc >450. Methadone is metabolized in the liver, and excreted into the gut; therefore, renal function is not a risk factor. Cognitive disorders and a history of substance abuse are not indicative of prolonging the QT interval, requiring a baseline EKG.

39. A) Obtain a urine drug screen and switch their morphine to MS Contin 30mg every 12 hours, with Morphine IR 5mg every 4 as needed.

Feedback: Since this is a newly diagnosed patient, they could be having uncontrolled pain issues. Obtaining a urine drug screen will show if they are actually taking the medication. Switching the patient to a longer acting morphine, such as MS Contin, with scheduled dosing and allowing for break through pain control with prn IR morphine, will allow the provider to further assess pain management and patient compliance. The patient can be exhibiting pseudo-addiction, which reflects behaviors of opioid abuse such as requesting early refills, but actually is a result of poorly controlled pain. If the patient is portraying pseudo-addiction, as soon as the pain is controlled the addictive behavior will stop.

40. B) Midazolam and lorazepam.

Feedback: Benzodiazepines, barbiturates, and mild general anesthesia is most commonly used for palliative sedation. Other medications include chlorpromazine, haloperidol, phenobarbital, thiopental, and propofol. Opioids are not typically used for palliative sedation.

Chapter 2

Scientific Knowledge: Practice Test 2

The scientific knowledge area of the test encompasses approximately 29% of the test. This portion of the test focuses on pathology, disease process, accurate diagnosis, and treatment options backed by evidence-based practice. The questions also cover what is considered an emergency in hospice and palliative care, and what is not. The psychology of loss and grief is also covered in this portion of the test. Ready, set, let's go!

41. Which patient is most eligible for hospice care?

    A) A 33 y/o patient with HIV who has a viral load >80,000, CD4+ >60 cells/mcl, PPS score of 60%, and a recent hospitalization for cryptosporidium infection.

    B) An 87-year-old patient with stage 4 lung cancer, a PPS score of 70%, serum calcium of 9, and a newly diagnosed liver lesion.

    C) A 76-year-old female with a history of dementia that cannot walk without assistance, speaks less than 6 intelligible words, and has recently been hospitalized for aspiration pneumonia.

    D) A 52 y/o male with end stage liver disease, severe abdominal pain, albumin level 3.5, INR 1.3, and has a DNR.

42. A normal serum calcium level is:

    A) 8.9-10.1.

    B) 1.5-3.5.

    C) 14-25.

    D) 35-45.

43. What type of cancer has the worst prognosis?

    A) Colon cancer.

    B) Pancreatic cancer.

    C) Breast cancer.

D) Prostate cancer.

44. Which patient is most likely experiencing end-of-dose failure:

A) A patient that has scheduled Percocet, three times a day, and states "I must be due for my next pain pill because my pain is getting really bad."

B) A patient on Vicodin that states, "I don't know why my doctor gives me these pills because they never do anything for me."

C) A patient that was recently started on a Fentanyl patch and states, "I have had this patch on for an entire day, and my pain keeps getting worse."

D) A patient on prn Percocet and states, "I'm going to take two instead of one next time."

45. Which drug has the most likelihood of causing QTc prolongation?

A) Methadone.

B) Percocet.

C) Hydromorphone.

D) Tramadol.

46. You are examining a patient with HIV and notice white patches on the sides of the patient's tongue. How do you treat this?

A) You realize this is an opportunistic bacterial infection and treat it with azithromycin.

B) You realize this is a side effect from the patient's antiviral therapy and know this is a chronic condition.

C) You realize this is a fungal infection and treat this with an antifungal medication such as nystatin.

D) You realize this is a viral infection and treat this with an oral swish and swallow antiviral medication.

47. A 68 y/o male with lung cancer has just completed chemotherapy and his recent lab results show an increased sed rate of 32, hgb 11, creatinine 1.4, and BUN 16. A probable diagnosis for this patient is:

    A) Fatigue.

    B) Inflammation.

    C) Anuresis.

    D) Dehydration.

48. What is the most significant indicator for decline in a patient with Alzheimer's?

    A) A decline in memory.

    B) A decline in function.

    C) A decline in appropriate behavior.

    D) An increase in UTI's.

49. Which medication will produce the fastest results for improving depression?

    A) Duloxetine.

    B) Sertraline.

    C) Eszopiclone.

    D) Methylphenidate.

50. Brain atrophy is seen on a CT scan. This can be suggestive of:

    A) Stroke.

    B) Dementia.

    C) ALS.

    D) Brain cancer.

51. You are examining a patient with lung cancer who has complaints of shortness of breath and a non-productive cough. On exam you notice dullness on percussion in the left lower lung base, as well as diminished breath sounds. You suspect:

  A) Superior vena cava obstruction.

  B) Pleural effusion.

  C) Cirrhosis with hepatic hydrothorax.

  D) CHF.

52. Kyphoplasty surgery is a procedure used to stop pain and stabilize bone caused by a spinal fracture, and is performed by:

  A) Injecting a cement-like material into the vertebrae.

  B) Removing the damaged vertebrae.

  C) Securely wiring the vertebrae.

  D) Replacing the vertebrae.

53. Which condition most likely indicates that cancer has spread to the bone causing bone breakdown?

  A) Anemia.

  B) Hyperkalemia.

  C) Hypercalcemia.

  D) Leukocytopenia.

54. What class of medications is typically given in the presence of hypercalcemia?

  A) Angiotensin Converting Enzyme Inhibitor (ACE).

  B) Selective Uric Acid Reabsorption Inhibitor (SURI).

  C) Biphosphonates.

D) Selective Serotonin Reuptake Inhibitor (SSRI).

55. What class of medications is considered first-line treatment for nausea and vomiting?

A) Anticholinergics.

B) Antihistamines.

C) Benzodiazepines.

D) Opioids.

56. Treatment for opioid-induced hyperalgesia (OIH) includes:

A) Reducing opioid dosages and starting ketamine.

B) Stopping all PO opioids and starting a fentanyl transdermal patch, since this route has been shown to decrease the likelihood of OIH.

C) Stopping all opioids and starting tramadol, in addition to a NSAID.

D) Calling 911, since this is considered a life-threatening condition.

57. What is the best definition for opioid-induced hyperalgesia (OIH)?

A) Nociceptive sensitization, caused by the exposure to opioids, characterized by a generalized hypersensitivity to pain, even in areas of the body that were not previously painful.

B) Nociceptive sensitization, caused by the exposure to opioids, characterized by a localized intensity of a refractory pain response.

C) Hypersensitivity response seen in opioid overuse.

D) A decrease in the effectiveness of opioids due to tolerance.

58. The best definition of allodynia is:

A) Pain produced by a non-noxious stimulus, or a pain response initiated by a previously non-painful stimulus.

B) Inability to feel pain.

C) A type of referred pain that spreads beyond the site of injury and diminishes once the original source of pain has been controlled.

D) A radiating pain that intensifies with movement and is often described as dull and achy.

59. The wife of a 62 y/o patient with lung cancer calls you crying because the patient is having difficulty breathing. She yells his face is beginning to swell up and "even his veins are showing!" You recognize the patient is most likely experiencing:

A) A progression of his cancer.

B) Superior vena cava syndrome.

C) Compartmental Syndrome.

D) Pericardial effusion.

60. A hospice patient with end-stage COPD is experiencing refractory dyspnea. Which medication would most likely be prescribed for symptom management for this patient?

A) Morphine.

B) Symbicort.

C) Atropine.

D) Lasix.

61. Cachexia differs from anorexia in all the following EXCEPT:

A) Cachexia occurs in the presence of metabolism alterations and the inability of the body to effectively use nutrients, despite adequate nutritional support, leading to wasting of bone mass and lean muscle tissue.

B) Nutritional support is ineffective in maintaining lean body mass with cachexia and is more inclined to increase primarily body fat.

C) High cytokine release and chronic inflammatory responses are associated with cachexia.

D) A low-protein diet is optimal for patients with cachexia.

62. First-line management for excessive secretions in an actively dying patient is:

A) Administration of an anticholinergic medication such as glycopyrrolate.

B) Bedside suction.

C) Repositioning of the patient, allowing for the drainage of secretions.

D) Raising the head of the bed to allow for improved air exchange.

63. A patient is having issues with insomnia and depression. What medication would be most appropriate to prescribe?

A) Mirtazapine.

B) Wellbutrin.

C) Zoloft.

D) Cymbalta.

64. Which medication would be best for families to have on hand for a patient with a high potential for seizures?

A) Valium 5mg PO.

B) Diazepam 5mg IV.

C) Diazepam 10mg rectal gel.

D) Valium 2.5mg SL.

65. Which person is most at risk for developing complicated grief?

A) An individual that has experienced previous loss, especially if it occurred in childhood.

B) An atheist.

C) A person that has a very limited support system.

D) Children less than 14 years of age.

66. A 76 y/o male died 18 months ago, and his widow calls you stating she still can't believe he is gone. She states she rarely leaves the house anymore, and she doesn't want to get out of bed in the morning. What is most important prior to hanging up:

A) Make a four week follow up.

B) Find a local grief support group.

C) Refer the patient to a bereavement counselor.

D) Find out her pharmacy information so you can call in a prescription for Zoloft.

67. A 54 y/o patient with metastatic breast cancer and a recent decline, calls you with concerns about her husband's behavior. She states he is no longer attentive and loving like he used to be and is rarely home anymore. He also hired a private caregiver instead of taking care of her himself like he used to. She says he seems to be distancing himself from her and "it's like he is just moving on with his life!" You realize that her husband is most likely experiencing:

A) Caregiver burnout.

B) Complicated grief.

C) Anticipatory grief.

D) Inadequate coping strategies.

68. What medication is often used in patients with ALS to control spasticity?

A) Baclofen.

B) Valium.

C) Soma.

D) Gabapentin.

69. A normal albumin level is:

    A) 3.6 – 5.1 g/dL.

    B) 8.6 – 10.4 mg/dL.

    C) 1.9 – 3.7 g/dL.

    D) 6 – 29 mg/dL.

70. Patients with end-stage liver disease and portal hypertension have an increased risk of:

    A) Bleeding from esophageal varices.

    B) Developing liver carcinoma.

    C) Developing malignant ascites.

    D) Increased ammonia levels.

71. The risk for spinal cord compression is highest in all of the following cancers EXCEPT:

    A) Pancreatic cancer.

    B) Breast cancer.

    C) Lung cancer.

    D) Prostate cancer.

72. A patient with hepatic cancer develops hemoptysis. What is the most likely cause?

    A) Platelet count of 40,000.

    B) Esophageal varices.

    C) Side effects of NSAID overuse.

    D) Vascular invasion from malignancy.

73. A patient with stage 3 breast cancer presents with complaints of severe back pain, new-onset numbness in her toes, as well as loss of bladder control. You immediately want to rule out:

A) Spinal cord compression.

B) Brain metastasis.

C) Metastasis to the lower extremities.

D) Metastasis to the liver.

74. Spinal cord compression most frequently occurs in which area of the spinal cord?

A) Cervical spine.

B) Lumbar spine.

C) Thoracic spine.

D) Sacral spine.

75. Studies show that men experience grief differently than women. For this reason, a therapist knows that men in a support group:

A) Must be prompted and encouraged to express their feelings of grief, because men are less likely to outwardly express emotion in this type of setting.

B) Are prone to make fun of those outwardly expressing their feelings, and the therapist will therefore need to set boundaries and rules in advance for group behavior.

C) Tend to take over and dominate the group and not allow others an opportunity to participate.

D) Tend to express grief in a more violent nature than women.

76. Calcium has a direct relationship with:

A) Creatinine.

B) Sodium.

C) Phosphate.

D) Albumin.

77. What condition indicates a worsening of CHF?

    A) Hyperkalemia.

    B) Hyponatremia.

    C) Hypercalcemia.

    D) Hypernatremia.

78. Signs of spiritual distress include:

    A) A patient stating, "I really don't belong to any type of organized religion, but I do consider myself spiritual."

    B) A patient stating, "I really don't know if I believe in God or not."

    C) A patient stating, "I really don't understand the bible."

    D) A patient stating, "I hate God. There is no purpose to life except to suffer."

79. What is evidence-based practice?

    A) Practice that is based on research.

    B) Practice that is based on theory.

    C) Practice that has sustained the test of time.

    D) Practice that is policy-based.

80. What is the recommended treatment for spinal cord compression?

    A) Radiation therapy.

    B) Surgical intervention.

    C) Steroid injection.

    D) Chemotherapy.

81. A 3rd heart sound is indicative of:

    A) Heart failure.

B) Cardiac arrhythmia.

C) Pericardial effusion.

D) Cardiac tamponade.

82. A patient had a stroke and has been in the neuro ICU for 3 days. An apnea test was performed to distinguish brain stem function. The results were absent respiration and a $PaCO_2$ of 80mmHg. You know this reflects:

A) A positive test for brain death.

B) A negative test for brain death.

C) Inconclusive, because this is a normal $PaCO_2$ level.

D) An EEG should be obtained since this is the gold standard.

83. What is the difference between a patient in a coma and a patient in a persistent vegetative state?

A) There is no difference. The terms are used interchangeably.

B) A coma patient is aware of their surroundings and can hear conversations but is unable to interact within their environment.

C) A patient in a persistent vegetative state has sleep-wake cycles.

D) A coma patient is unconscious for a prolonged period of time but can be awakened by stimulation.

84. A patient with end-stage liver disease is having increased confusion. He has been taking his lactulose and having bowel movements regularly. He is having nausea, dark-colored urine, decreased urine output, weight gain, and is jaundiced. Which lab test should be ordered:

A) Ammonia level.

B) Creatinine.

C) Albumin.

D) LFTs.

85. A ketamine infusion for OIH works by affecting which receptors?

A) Gamma-aminobutyric acid (GABA) receptors.

B) Dopamine receptors.

C) N-methyl-D-aspartate (NMDA) receptors.

D) Opioid kappa receptors.

86. A patient with end-stage liver disease is icteric and has complaints of severe itching. Which medication should be tried first to alleviate his symptoms of pruritus?

A) Hydrocortisone cream.

B) An antihistamine such as Benadryl.

C) Naloxone.

D) A bile resin binder such as cholestyramine.

87. A 62 y/o male with stage 4 metastatic lung cancer has complaints of extreme fatigue that is affecting his quality of life. Which intervention would be most helpful in relieving his symptoms?

A) Methylphenidate.

B) Sertraline.

C) Caffeine.

D) A good exercise program.

Pearls for Passing

- This type of patient population typically has several issues occurring simultaneously. Cases will be presented with many different issues occurring concurrently and you will need to determine what the question is really asking. For example, a patient can present with a history of CHF, kidney failure, chronic pain, and anxiety. The family calls you, stating the patient is crying and saying they cannot breathe. Focus on what information the question is giving you and what issue they are actually focusing on.

- Know what constitutes an emergency in hospice care. The goal is not to prolong life, but to prolong function and quality. Think function = quality.

- Know how the body and mind respond to grief. Know the different types of grief and how they present clinically. Know what puts some people at a higher risk of dysfunctional grieving than others.

- Know how to assess common cancer-related issues such as a pleural effusion, and with which types of cancers this is most commonly associated with.

- Know the most frequently seen diagnoses in hospice care, such as COPD, cancer, end-stage liver disease, end-stage renal disease, heart failure, and Alzheimer's. Know what makes each of these diagnoses eligible for hospice care.

- Know how to assess for dehydration. Know what labs to order and how to read them.

- There will be many scenarios which will require lab interpretation. If a lab is *slightly* abnormal, that is typically not the major issue going on.

- Know treatment options for persistent hiccups that will not go away (a quality of life issue).

- Know the difference between cachexia and anorexia. Does giving a patient nutritional supplements help the issue of cachexia?

- Know why some wounds will not heal so you can give realistic expectations to the patient and family.
- Know how to manage a patient during a seizure.
- Know the causes for urinary retention and how to treat it.
- Know how a patient with dementia presents with a UTI. Hint: Think behavioral changes and non-verbal behaviors associated with pain.
- Know the quickest method of treating depression in a person with only weeks to live. Hint: Think stimulant.
- Know which chronic disease has a long illness trajectory with multiple exacerbations, frequent hospital admissions, and then a quick downward progression toward death.
- Know what the deadliest cancer is, with the poorest prognosis: pancreatic cancer.
- Know what a left ventricular assist device (LVAD) is, and its limitations.
- Remember the stages of grief, not only for the patient, but for the family. Anger and denial are part of these stages, so when families exhibit these behaviors it is best to address them as they come up, ie: family meetings.
- Know how the body reacts during the dying process and what to expect.

Practice Test 2: Answers and Rationales

41. C) A 76 y/o female with a history of dementia that cannot walk without assistance, speaks less than 6 intelligible words, and has recently been hospitalized for aspiration pneumonia.

Feedback: Hospice eligibility for dementia requires Stage 7C or below, according to the FAST scale, as well as one or more qualifiers such as aspiration pneumonia. Hospice eligibility for liver disease includes a PT>5 sec, or an INR >1.5, serum albumin <2.5 gm/dl, and one or more qualifiers such as refractory ascites or hepatorenal syndrome. Hospice eligibility for a cancer diagnosis includes a PPS score ≤ 70%, and hypercalcemia >12. Hospice eligibility for HIV includes CD4+ <25 cells/mcl, or a viral load >100,000, and a PPS score of <50%.

42. A) 8.9-10.1.

Feedback: Normal calcium levels range from 8.9-10.1, with a slight variance depending on the lab. None of the other answer's correspond with normal serum calcium levels.

43. B) Pancreatic cancer.

Feedback: Regardless of the stage pancreatic cancer is diagnosed at, the 1-year survival rate is 20%, and the 5-year survival rate is 7%. Pancreatic cancer is still largely considered incurable. Colon, breast, and prostate cancer have much higher survival rates.

44. A) A patient that has scheduled Percocet, three times a day, and states "I must be due for my next pain pill because my pain is getting really bad."

Feedback: The goal of pain management for patients with chronic pain issues is to keep their pain controlled for 24 hours. With adequate pain control, the patient should not be waking up in the middle of the night secondary to pain or glued to their watch because they are in pain and their next pill is not due for another hour. End-of-dose failure refers to patients taking a scheduled dose of a narcotic and the relief not lasting until the next pill is due.

45. A) Methadone.

Feedback: Methadone has been associated with QTc prolongation. An EKG should be obtained prior to starting the medication in patients with a cardiac history.

46. C) You realize this is a fungal infection and treat this with an antifungal medication such as nystatin.

Feedback: Candidiasis is a fungal infection seen in the mouth, throat, and esophagus and occurs due to compromised immunity. It is treated with an antifungal medication such as nystatin for 10-14 days.

47. A) Fatigue.

Feedback: Fatigue is one of the most common side effects of cancer treatment. Studies have shown a relationship of fatigue among chemotherapy patients with hgb levels <12. It is not unusual to find increased sed rates in patients with cancer or arthritis. The patient is not dehydrated, and signs of fatigue do not typically occur until stage 3 kidney failure.

48. B) A decline in function.

Feedback: Eligibility for hospice care in patients with dementia is primarily based on function. On the FAST scale, a score of 7C is required. This means the patient is unable to ambulate without assistance, unable to dress or bathe without assistance, has urinary and fecal incontinence, and cognitive function has declined to the point where the patient can speak fewer than 6 words. A decline in memory has to be substantiated by a demonstration of cognitive ability, such as verbal articulation. Inappropriate behavior such as hitting or acting out, does not necessarily mean the patient has less than 6 months to live, nor do repeated UTI's.

49. D) Methylphenidate.

Feedback: Methylphenidate (Ritalin) is a stimulant and works very quickly, having a half-life of 3.5 hours. Beneficial results with SSRIs such as Serotonin (Zoloft), and SNRI's such as Duloxetine (Cymbalta), are not seen for 6 to 8 weeks. Eszopiclone (Lunesta) is for insomnia.

50. B) Dementia.

Feedback: Brain atrophy is part of normal aging, but the rate of atrophy is accelerated in individuals with Alzheimer's disease. Studies have found patients with Alzheimer's disease can have 3 to 4% brain loss in a year, whereas loss of brain tissue secondary to atrophy with normal aging was <1% a year.

51. B) Pleural effusion.

Feedback: Pleural effusions are common in patients with lung cancer and is often the first presenting symptom. Patient's usually present with dyspnea and a non-productive cough. A CT scan is typically ordered. Superior vena cava obstruction, cirrhosis with hepatic hydrothorax, and CHF are all considered differential diagnoses for a pleural effusion, but clinical judgment is usually a good indicator.

52. A) Injecting a cement-like material into the vertebrae.

Feedback: Kyphoplasty is a very simple surgical procedure that can be done with local or mild general anesthesia. It is done using fluoroscopy and a cement-like material that hardens very quickly called polymethylmethacrylate, and is injected into the fractured area of the vertebrae. This stabilizes the fracture and reduces pain.

53. C) Hypercalcemia.

Feedback: When cancer spreads to the bone and erodes bone tissue, calcium is released into the blood causing hypercalcemia. Although anemia and variations in white blood cell counts will occur in the presence of cancer, the question is specifically asking about the effects of bone erosion. Potassium levels are not an indication of bone breakdown, and typically reflects other causes such as renal disease.

54. C) Bisphosphonates.

Feedback: Bisphosphates prevent osteoclast-mediated bone loss in the occurrence of hypercalcemia in malignancies. Selective uric acid reabsorption inhibitors (SURI) are a new class of anti-gout medications. SSRI's and ACE Inhibitors are not appropriate.

55. A) Anticholinergics.

Feedback: Anticholinergics block the neurotransmitter acetylcholine, and inhibit the transmission of parasympathetic nerve impulses, which reduces spasms of smooth muscles. This class of medications has considerable side effects such as dry mouth, urinary retention, delirium, dilated pupils, tachycardia, flushing of skin, and constipation.

56. A) Reducing opioid dosage and starting ketamine.

Feedback: OIH involves the activation of N-methyl D-aspartate (NMDA) receptors, therefore pharmacological approaches work to block these receptors with antagonists such as ketamine, in addition to opioid reduction. All other answers are not indicated for treatment of OIH.

57. A) Nociceptive sensitization caused by the exposure to opioids is characterized by a generalized hypersensitivity to pain, even in areas of the body that were not previously painful.

Feedback: Opioid-induced hyperalgesia (OIH) is a paradoxical response to opioids, where the patient encounters a more intense pain response affecting areas outside of the initial area of pain. For example, a continual increase in opioids is given to a patient for left femur pain. Her pain escalates with increasing opioid dosages to the point that even a light back rub causes the patient severe discomfort. An overuse of opioids is incorrect because opioid-naïve patients can encounter OIH. It is typically seen with frequent and escalating dose changes. A localized intensity of pain is more indicative of Complex Regional Pain Syndrome (CRPS). Opioid overdose presents with a decrease in arousal and respiration, not an increase in hypersensitivity.

58. A) Pain produced by a non-noxious stimulus, or a pain response initiated by a previously non-painful stimulus.

Feedback: Allodynia is characterized as pain caused by a stimulus that normally does not produce pain such as light touch. Most people describe allodynia as feeling like pinpricks or a burning sensation. Although allodynia occurs in areas other than the original source of pain, it is not considered "radiating," such as pain associated with cardiac issues, nor is it considered "referred," such as pain related to an appendicitis.

59. B) Superior vena cava syndrome.

Feedback: Superior vena cava syndrome commonly occurs in the presence of chest cancer's that have grown, causing compression of the superior vena cava. Typical signs include facial edema, dyspnea, and vein distention. Although disease progression has most likely occurred, the reason for this patient's symptoms are due to compression of the superior vena cava. Facial edema is not a clinical indicator for a pericardial effusion. Compartment syndrome is incorrect because this typically occurs after an injury and causes excessive pressure build-up inside an enclosed muscle.

60. A) Morphine.

Feedback: For refractory dyspnea, low-dose opioids have been shown to reduce symptoms when optimal therapy for the underlying condition have been exhausted. A hospice patient with end-stage COPD has most likely exhausted conventional management for COPD, and studies have shown a significant reduction in symptoms with the use of opioids for refractory dyspnea in this population of patients.

61. D) A low-protein diet is optimal for patients with cachexia.

Feedback: Cachexia is also known as "wasting syndrome," and is a condition in which the body can no longer adequately use food sources to maintain sustenance due to alterations in metabolism, (which often increases with cancer), and a chronic inflammatory response secondary to the disease process. This is seen in the late stages of a disease and is not reversible and does not respond to supplementation. Despite giving the patient a high-protein diet secondary to muscle atrophy, supplementation primarily turns to fat instead of muscle, and the patient continues to lose lean muscle mass and bone.

62. C) Repositioning of the patient, allowing for the drainage of secretions.

Feedback: First-line management for addressing excessive secretions in actively dying patients is to reposition the patient's head to allow for secretions to drain naturally. A washcloth can be placed for absorption. Aggressive suctioning is ineffective and has been found to produce even more secretions. Anticholinergics such as glycopyrrolate are given when other management methods have failed. Anticholinergics are not always effective.

63. A) Mirtazapine.

Feedback: Mirtazapine is often given for insomnia and depression. It is best to give one pill that can treat several issues and is cost-effective.

64. C) Diazepam 10mg rectal gel.

Feedback: Never give anything PO to a patient having an active seizure. For the families of hospice patients, it is not practical to have IV medications on hand since most patients on home hospice do not have IV access. Rectal diazepam is available as a rectal gel in prefilled syringes called Diastat.

65. A) An individual that has experienced previous loss, especially if it occurred in childhood.

Feedback: Some risk factors for complicated grief include a history of mental illness, substance abuse, previous loss, and sudden unexpected death. A child, a loner, or an atheist does not necessarily set the stage for complicated grief, although bereavement counseling should be available and encouraged.

66. B) Find a local grief support group.

Feedback: Medicare pays for bereavement counseling for up to 1 year after the patient's death. Additional grief counseling would then be through a local support group. Since she is not your patient and you have not evaluated her, you should suggest she make an appointment with her PCP for evaluation and medication needs.

67. C) Anticipatory grief.

Feedback: Her husband is most likely experiencing anticipatory grief. The patient's recent decline in condition and the reality of her death becomes more imminent. Emotional numbness and fear are signs of anticipatory grief. Caregiver burnout typically presents with feelings of irritability, fatigue, and loss of empathy. Grief is a normal process and is not considered inadequate coping. The grieving process does not always start at the moment of the patient's death and can often present at the time of diagnosis or during periods of decline.

68. A) Baclofen.

Feedback: Muscle spasms frequently occur in patients with ALS and are typically controlled with a muscle relaxant such as baclofen.

69. A) 3.6 - 5.1 g/dL.

Feedback: Normal albumin levels range between 3.6 - 5.1 g/dL, with a slight variance depending on the lab running the test. None of the other answers represent normal albumin ranges.

70. A) Bleeding from esophageal varices.

Feedback: Portal hypertension often occurs in the presence of cirrhosis. Increased intrahepatic vascular resistance, and increased blood flow through the portal venous system, leads to the development of portosystemic collateral veins. With medium to large veins in the esophagus, the patient has up to a 30% chance of bleeding out within two years.

71. A) Pancreatic cancer.

Feedback: Any type of cancer can spread to the spine, but it is more commonly associated with: breast cancer, lung cancer, prostate cancer, kidney cancer, lymphoma, and multiple-myeloma. Up to 70% of spinal cord compression, secondary to the spread of malignancies, occurs in the thoracic spine area. The most common symptom is back pain. Radiation therapy is the treatment of choice.

72. D) Vascular invasion of malignancy.

Feedback: Bleeding often occurs when cancer spreads and invades vascular tissue. This is the most likely reason the patient is experiencing hemoptysis, especially in relation to the other answer choices. Bleeding typically does not occur with thrombocytopenia until the platelet count reaches 20,000 or below. There is no mention of pulmonary hypertension, ascites, or the use of NSAIDs, so remember not to make more of what a question is asking.

73. A) Spinal cord compression.

Feedback: Tumor growth can cause pressure on the spinal cord causing cord compression, and is most often seen with breast, lung, and prostate carcinomas. The presenting symptoms and history are not congruent with brain, liver, or lower extremity metastasis.

74. C) Thoracic spine.

Feedback: Seventy percent of metastatic invasion to the spine occurs at the thoracic region, particularly between T4-T7, and most often occurs with lung and breast cancer as the primary source. The other answers are statistically incorrect.

75. A) Must be prompted and encouraged to express their feelings of grief, because men are less likely to outwardly express emotion in this type of setting.

Feedback: Studies have shown that men are less likely than women to openly express emotions or openly cry. This is felt to be a reflection of social norms for males having to show strength, and crying being perceived as a sign of weakness. Men often prefer to grieve alone or in private. The other answers are incorrect and do not reflect how men typically grieve.

76. C) Phosphate.

Feedback: Calcium has a direct relationship with phosphorus and regulate homeostasis of each other. As blood calcium levels rise, phosphate levels fall. Albumin, creatinine, and sodium do not have the homeostatic relationship of calcium and phosphorus.

77. B) Hyponatremia.

Feedback: Antidiuretic hormone release and the reduction in serum sodium, correlate with the severity of heart failure. The other answers do not have a direct correlation with the severity of heart failure.

78. D) A patient stating, "I hate God. There is no purpose to life except to suffer."

Feedback: Spiritual distress involves an anger toward God and a loss of meaning in life. The other answers do not show anger toward God or a loss of purpose.

79. A) Practice that is based on research.

Feedback: Evidence-based practice is based on research that has proven outcomes. Some research is conducted through qualitative methods, where the researcher gathers data by observation or in written or verbal formats such as interviews and surveys. Quantitative research is primarily conducted in a laboratory or well-controlled environment, relying on statistical data.

80. A) Radiation therapy.

Feedback: Radiation therapy is first-line treatment for spinal cord compression and should be initiated within 24 hours of diagnosis. Radiation quickly relieves pressure on the spinal cord by shrinking the tumor. Quality of life is of utmost importance and the ability to preserve function. Steroids can be given in conjunction with radiation therapy, but they do not achieve substantial immediate results. Radiation therapy is a non-invasive symptom relief measure, and surgical options are typically avoided.

81. A) Heart failure.

Feedback: A 3rd heart sound is indicative of increased ventricular filling and is found in congestive heart failure and with severe mitral or tricuspid regurgitation. S3 is usually faint and lower in pitch than S1 and S2. A pericardial effusion is associated with a pericardial friction rub which sounds high-pitched, scratching, or grating on auscultation. Cardiac tamponade is evidenced by tachycardia, diminished heart sounds, and a pericardial friction rub. Hearing a 3rd heart sound is not considered an arrhythmia and can be considered a normal finding in certain patient populations.

82. A) A positive test for brain death.

Feedback: Brain death is generally determined at bedside and made by clinical assessment. The apnea test is a frequently used evaluation tool for testing brain stem function. The absence of a drive to breathe is tested with a CO_2 challenge. An apnea test is considered positive when no breathing effort is observed at a $PaCO_2$ level of 60mmHg, or with a 20mmHg increase from baseline. There is no gold standard for making the diagnosis for brain death. EEGs are not typically done for confirmation due to artifacts. Normal $PaCO_2$ range is 35-45mmHg.

83. C) A patient in a persistent vegetative state has sleep-wake cycles.

Feedback: One of the primary differences is a patient in a persistent vegetative state has sleep-wake cycles. In a coma, the patient is unconscious and unresponsive. A patient in a persistent vegetative state is conscious but has lost cognitive function. A good example is the Terri Schiavo case in which she had sleep and wake cycles and was conscious. Her caregivers felt that she had purposeful awareness of them and her surroundings. In actuality, she had no purposeful connection with her environment due to the severity of her brain damage as was evidenced by the MRI of her brain. The prognosis for a patient in a coma depends on the underlying cause and severity of the brain damage. Patients in a persistent vegetative state have a very low chance of recovery after the first 6 months.

84. B) Creatinine.

Feedback: Hepatorenal syndrome is a common disorder that occurs in approximately 40% of patients with end-stage liver disease. Symptoms can be vague, and the patient's renal failure can be overshadowed by the patient's end-stage liver disease. A creatinine level should be checked if a decrease in urine output is evidenced, and will assist in the diagnosis of hepatorenal syndrome. Ammonia levels should be drawn when ruling out hepatic encephalopathy. Due to the patient taking his lactulose and having regular bowel movements, it would be wise to explore other reasons for the patient's clinical presentation. There is no point in drawing LFTs or albumin level when you are looking to primarily rule out renal failure.

85. C) N-methyl-D-aspartate (NMDA) receptors.

Feedback: The NMDA receptors are the primary binding site for ketamine, which is an NMDA antagonist. Ketamine acts as an agonist on dopamine, opioid kappa, and GABA receptors.

86. D) A bile resin binder such as cholestyramine.

Feedback: The recommended approach for treating pruritus in end-stage liver disease is to first try bile resin binders, followed by rifampin, and then naltrexone for the possibility of buildup of endogenous opioids. Antihistamines are not effective in treating cholestatic pruritus. Hydrocortisone cream is used for localized inflammatory conditions.

87. A) Methylphenidate.

Feedback: Methylphenidate is a CNS stimulant and has been shown to improve symptoms of fatigue in cancer patients. SSRI's are not used to treat fatigue. Caffeine will most likely be ineffective and can cause adverse reactions if taken in excess. This patient would not be able to tolerate a strenuous exercise program, so this option is unrealistic.

Chapter 3

Education & Communication Test 3

The education and communication portion of the examination encompasses approximately 17% of the test. This portion of the test focuses on adult learning, communication, advance care planning, and how to have discussions regarding difficult subject matter. Ready, set, let's go!

88. A 22 y/o Korean female is hospitalized for renal failure. She is alert and oriented and tells the nurse that she is extremely concerned about having to have dialysis. Her family is very involved in her care, and her mother approaches you asking if something else could be done other than dialysis. In this culture, who is known for making healthcare decisions?

A) The family.

B) The husband, father, or eldest son.

C) The mother or wife, since females are considered the caregivers.

D) The patient, if age appropriate, and if they are able to make healthcare decisions for themselves.

89. What are some of the most important components of an advance directive?

A) Assigning a healthcare proxy to make healthcare decisions when the patient can no longer do so for themselves.

B) Delegating assets prior to an individual's death.

C) Ensuring post-mortem religious beliefs have been carried out.

D) Assigning a power of attorney over your will.

90. Many PCPs are referring their patients with chronic pain issues to palliative care. All of the following can be put into place to decrease the abuse of opioids EXCEPT:

A) Routine urine testing, opioid contracts, and risk assessment tools.

B) Making patients aware they cannot refill their medications early if they run out or lose their medication.

C) Having the patient tell the provider what opioid works best for them and what amount.

D) Having the patient call the provider if the pain medication is not working, and have them bring in their medication so the provider can see how much they have taken.

91. Some patients require very frequent blood transfusions due to certain anemias and cancers. It is appropriate to stop receiving blood transfusions at the end-of-life for all of the following EXCEPT:

A) When the patient's goals of care have been reviewed and the primary goal is comfort.

B) When the burden of invasive treatments outweighs the benefits.

C) When blood transfusions show no improvement in fatigue or survival.

D) When the patient is at high risk for hemorrhage.

92. While evaluating a patient for hospice the family approaches you very upset stating the patient's oncologist said they had at least two years to live, and do not understand why you (hospice) are there. Upon your eval, you can clearly see the patient has less than 6 months to live, and hospice is appropriate. You review oncology's notes and the chart confirms the family's statement stating a prognosis of two years. What do you do?

A) Apologize to the family and pretend you have the wrong patient.

B) Schedule a meeting with oncology to further discuss the patient's case.

C) Tell the family the oncologist was wrong.

D) Recognize this as an overestimated prognosis secondary to the family wanting aggressive treatment.

93. What does the acronym GOLD mean in relation to COPD?

A) Global Initiative for Chronic Obstructive Lung Disease (GOLD).

B) Glandular Obstructive Lung Disease (GOLD).

C) Genetic Obstructive Lung Disease (GOLD).

D) Gold Standard for Obstructive Lung Disease (GOLD).

94. Reasons why wounds do not heal in hospice patients include all of the following EXCEPT:

A) Poor tissue perfusion.

B) Poor nutritional status.

C) Decreased functional status.

D) Limited ability of the family to care for the patient's wounds.

95. A patient has been receiving dialysis for end-stage renal failure for many years and tells you they want to stop because they have had enough. The patient has a living will, signed DNR, and has appointed their son as the healthcare proxy. After several days, the patient becomes confused and lethargic. The son states he is the healthcare proxy and "I cannot just let my father die." He tells you he wants to reverse the DNR and restart his father's dialysis. You should:

A) Call a family meeting and allow the son to express his emotions and concerns.

B) Tell the son that his father trusted him to carry out his wishes.

C) Explain to him what a healthcare proxy is, and inform him that he is breaking his father's trust in him.

D) Call bereavement and have them counsel the son.

96. The most appropriate thing to say when someone has died is:

A) "They are in a better place."

B) "You won't be able to see them anymore, but at least you've got memories."

C) "I'm sorry for your loss."

D) "Well at least now they aren't suffering and in all of that pain anymore!"

97. The term "medical futility" means:

    A) There is no beneficial reason to start or continue a given treatment or procedure.

    B) There is a medical benefit that outweighs the risk of a treatment or procedure.

    C) There is an equal benefit to risk ratio, therefore it is up to the patient if they want to proceed with a treatment or procedure.

    D) Their risk outweighs the benefits of a procedure or treatment.

98. A physician enters a patient's room to discuss a patient's disease trajectory and prognosis. He starts by asking the patient what they already know about their illness, and to what detail they would feel comfortable discussing it. The physician is using a communication technique called:

    A) Ask-Tell-Ask communication technique.

    B) Linear communication.

    C) Permissive communication.

    D) Authoritarian communication.

99. What is the difference between capacity and competence?

    A) A patient's decision-making capacity can be determined by a medical professional, while competency must be determined by the courts.

    B) Competency can be determined by medical professionals, while capacity must be determined by the courts.

    C) A patient would have to be referred to psychiatry and be diagnosed as incompetent, while a patient's decision-making capacity could be determined at bedside.

    D) Only a physician can deem a patient incompetent.

100. Which person is most at risk for opioid abuse or misuse?

   A) A person with chronic pain issues.

   B) A family history of substance abuse.

   C) A person with cognitive impairment.

   D) Patients between the ages of 50 and 80.

Pearls
for
Passing

- ϕ̈ Know how to be aware of when communicating with a translator.
- ϕ̈ Know how to educate a patient and/or family, and how to evaluate their understanding afterward.
- ϕ̈ Know how to educate patients and families regarding the difference between palliative care and hospice care.
- ϕ̈ Know the communication method called "Ask, Tell, Ask."
- ϕ̈ Know what a teachable moment is, and when to let the moment pass. For example, if you just told the patient they have a prognosis of three months to live, it would not be appropriate to immediately attempt to educate them on advanced directives and have them sign a DNR.
- ϕ̈ Know how and when to approach patients regarding organ donation.
- ϕ̈ Know what can affect communication such as education levels, hearing impairments, cultural norms such as eye contact, invading personal space, and body language.
- ϕ̈ Know what to do when families do not want you to tell the patient their prognosis.
- ϕ̈ Know when the best time is to implement a referral for palliative care.
- ϕ̈ Prior to starting a discussion with a patient regarding their disease trajectory, first assess what they already know.
- ϕ̈ Know what verbiage to use when a patient has died. It has been found that healthcare providers should use the word "died" when a patient death has occurred.

- When conducting an interview with a patient in which you are trying to obtain information, use open-ended questions to help elicit communication.
- Always acknowledge and validate a person's emotions. For example, "I can see this is making you upset."
- Expect conflict and know how to negotiate conflict resolution.
- One of the most important elements of an advance directive is having the patient appoint a trusted individual to make medical decisions for them when they cannot. This person should be the one who knows the patient best and has been told by the patient what they want. Some advance directives are not as specific as others, so this individual should have a good idea of the patient's wishes. Advance directives do not contain information regarding religious practices or postmortem care.
- Advance directives are of utmost importance with ALS patients. Communication can become very difficult for them and a healthcare surrogate should be obtained as soon as possible.
- Know that heart failure is the number one killer in the United States, followed by cancer.
- Know that stroke does not equal dementia.
- Know how to determine a patient's decision-making capacity. Know that only the courts can declare a patient "incompetent."

88. B) The husband, father, or eldest son.

Feedback: In the Korean culture, the husband, father, or eldest son ultimately makes the decisions, although the family is typically very involved in the patient's care. This culture is family-focused, although the husband, father, or eldest son will most likely have the final say.

89. A) Assigning a healthcare proxy to make healthcare decisions when you can no longer do so for yourself.

Feedback: The purpose of advance directives is to have a way to voice your healthcare wishes when you can no longer do so. A healthcare proxy is an individual that is assigned by the patient to make healthcare decisions on their behalf. The healthcare proxy should be aware of what the patient's wishes are, and this individual is being trusted to carry out those wishes. A power of attorney over an individual's will and delegation of assets is not part of the components of an advance directive. Religious beliefs such as post-mortem rituals can be carried out by the healthcare proxy, but this is not one of the primary components such as life-sustaining measures.

90. C) Having the patient tell the provider what opioid works best for them and what amount.

Feedback: Avenues can be obtained to help reduce the occurrence of drug diversion. Unfortunately, no matter what providers do to ensure the safety of opioid prescriptions, there is no way of fully knowing what goes on after the drugs are dispensed to the patient. For this reason, providers should be able to recognize certain behaviors that are red flags for opioid abuse and misuse. Patients that dictate to the provider exactly what opioid they want and how many milligrams, while stating all other medications do not work for them is highly indicative of a person knowing exactly what the street value is for a certain type of drug.

91. D) When the patient is at high risk for hemorrhage.

Feedback: Unfortunately, some patients are at high risk of hemorrhage at the end-of-life. When the burden of invasive procedures outweighs the benefits, and the patient's goals of care are comfort, the possibility of hemorrhage must be taken into consideration and addressed. Using dark towels and bedding helps family members cope who are present at the bedside. For hematemesis or hemoptysis, placing the patient in the lateral position is recommended.

92. B) Schedule a meeting with oncology to further discuss the patient's case.

Feedback: Upholding a good relationship with your referral source and discussing referred cases is not only expected but is an important aspect for transparency in managing the care of the patients being referred. Either call oncology or set up a meeting for further discussion. While it is known that families and those close to the individual with a terminal illness frequently overestimate the possibility for a cure, it is good practice to review or correlate what the family is telling you with the chart or the referring provider. Terminal illnesses reach a point where life-sustaining methods are no longer an option and quality of life is the primary focus.

93. A) Global Initiative for Chronic Obstructive Lung Disease (GOLD).

Feedback: In 1998, the Global Initiative for Chronic Obstructive Lung Disease (GOLD) was formed to educate and help set universal standards of treatment. In 2014, the GOLD report published an individualized approach to COPD classification and management, as well as a review of how these interventions improve outcomes and/or quality of life.

94. D) Limited ability of the family to care for the patient's wounds.

Feedback: Poor tissue perfusion due to pathological changes in perfusion at the end-of-life prevent wound healing. Other factors include poor nutritional intake, especially protein sources, and poor functional status, resulting in poor pressure relief measures. The family's ability to care for wounds in dying patients is typically not a reason for a wound's inability to heal.

95. A) Call a family meeting and allow the son to express his emotions.

Feedback: Addressing the emotional concerns of the son is of utmost importance and coordinating a family meeting allowing for a supportive environment in which this can occur. Explaining what a healthcare proxy is or accusing the son of breaking his father's trust prior to addressing the son's immediate emotional state, can further heighten the stressors surrounding the situation.

96. C) "I'm sorry for your loss."

Feedback: All you want to do is acknowledge the death and give your condolences. By simply stating, "I am sorry for your loss," you have accomplished this without the possibility of offending anyone or accidentally hurting them further.

97. A) There is no beneficial reason to start or continue a given treatment or procedure.

Feedback: Medical futility is when there is no benefit for a treatment or procedure. An example is a patient that is brain dead and on a ventilator. It is medically futile to keep the patient on the ventilator.

98. A) Ask-Tell-Ask communication technique.

Feedback: The Ask-Tell-Ask technique starts the dialogue by first asking the patient what they already know about their illness. This gives the provider insight as to what the patient already knows. This is important information because the patient may have the idea that further treatment or a cure is still available for their condition. The patient must first come to a realization that their illness has progressed far beyond a viable cure or treatment option before end-of-life discussions can effectively be held. Linear communication is one-way, such as communication from a newspaper or TV. Authoritarian communication is power-assertive, controlling, and highly unidirectional. Permissive communication has few boundaries, minimal control, and is indulgent. These styles of communication are not viewed as effective or therapeutic in delivering news of terminal illness.

99. A) A patient's decision-making capacity can be determined by a medical professional, while competency must be determined by the courts.

Feedback: A court determines if a patient is incompetent to make medical decisions, and when necessary, a court-appointed representative will then be in charge of making these decisions for the patient. Assessing capacity can easily be done by medical professionals. A patient signing a consent form should be able to verbalize understanding and purpose of a procedure, as well as the risks and benefits associated with it. They should also be able to verbalize consequences of not having a procedure if refusing. Only courts can deem a patient as incompetent. Decision-making capacity can be assessed by medical professionals.

100. B) A family history of substance abuse.

Feedback: Risk factors include a family history of substance abuse, since genetics play a role in addictive behaviors. Other risk factors include personal history of substance abuse, ages between 16 and 45, history of preadolescent sexual abuse, and psychological disorders such ADD, OCD, bipolar, schizophrenia, and depression. The Opioid Risk Tool (ORT) can be used for risk assessment prior to prescribing. The other answers are not risk factors for opioid abuse or misuse.

Chapter 4

Professionalism: Practice Test 4

The topic of professionalism encompasses approximately 13% of the examination. This portion of the test focuses on scope of practice, leadership, ethics surrounding assisted suicide, palliative sedation, and withdrawing life-sustaining therapies. Let's see how you do!

101. The referring physician tells the nurse that he prefers to keep his patients in their homes as much as possible. He instructs the nurse to start performing paracentesis procedures on end-stage liver disease patients in their homes to reduce the need for frequent hospitalizations. What should the nurse do?

   A) Do as the physician tells you and add paracentesis to your collaborative agreement.

   B) Check with your state's scope of practice prior to proceeding.

   C) State you would be happy to if the physician showed you how to perform them.

   D) Tell the physician that a paracentesis cannot be performed in patient's home.

102. A colleague has been working two jobs for over a year and states, "all I do is take care of patients from the time I wake up to the time I go to bed." Which behavior would be most concerning and indicative for burnout?

   A) A colleague starts crying at the death of a patient.

   B) A colleague yells at a nurse stating she is incompetent.

   C) A colleague says "I've got to get out of here. I'm taking my family on a two-week vacation."

   D) A colleague comments that she is tired of trying to educate her patients, when they ignore her and do what they want anyway.

103. You want to make a policy change that will directly affect your colleagues. The best way to successfully implement this change and gain your colleagues buy-in would be to:

A) Plan a retreat allowing for open discussion outside of the work environment.

B) Have a meeting with your colleagues informing them of the change and the planned implementation date.

C) Implement the change and expect emotional flexibility, since change is inevitable in any organization.

D) Tell your colleagues that the change was mandated by upper management and you had no choice.

104. The ethical principle that refers to truth telling is called:

A) Veracity.

B) Non-maleficence.

C) Justice.

D) Beneficence.

105. How long is a patient's health record considered confidential after their death?

A) After a person has died, their health record is no longer considered confidential.

B) A patient's health record remains confidential for up to 5 years after they have died.

C) A patient's health record remains confidential for up to 50 years after they have died.

D) A patient's health record remains confidential for up to 3 years after they have died.

106. A colleague is having a difficult time balancing family and work. You suggest:

A) Taking a vacation.

B) Cutting back to part-time.

C) Mindfulness training.

D) Cognitive-behavioral training.

107. When would an ethics consult be appropriate?

A) When the family disagrees with the patient's wishes.

B) When a family conflict is putting undue pressure on a healthcare surrogate.

C) When a patient decides they no longer want to be on life-sustaining treatments.

D) When a family is demanding life-sustaining treatment for an unconscious patient for their own financial benefit of keeping them alive.

108. A hospice patient with a history of substance abuse has tested positive for marijuana. You tell them that you will no longer write them prescriptions for their opioids because of this. The provider may now be at risk for all of the following EXCEPT:

A) Withholding of medical care or treatment.

B) Not adhering to the ANA's goal of hospice and palliative nursing care.

C) Breaking the ethical principle of non-maleficence (do no harm) secondary to withholding the patients pain medications.

D) Responsible behavior by the provider, since it is their license and their decision.

109. A patient with ALS is on hospice care and has now reached an end point in their disease process. Non-invasive approaches are no longer sustaining their symptoms of dyspnea. The family and patient are now asking for tracheotomy placement with mechanical ventilation. Your response should include all of the following EXCEPT:

A) Explain that mechanical ventilation will not stop the disease process, and the patient would then have an increased chance of becoming "locked-in."

B) Discuss the issue further in a team meeting involving the patient and family. Inform the patient and family if they decide to pursue this change in the patient's plan of care, the patient can no longer be on hospice.

C) Support the patient's autonomy and family's request, but make sure they understand what the procedure entails, as well as the patient's inability to communicate. Discuss the effects on the patient's quality of life and the potential consequences of their decision.

D) Deny the request because this would require respiratory therapy, and hospice does not provide this type of support.

110. You are in the process of being credentialed for a hospital in your local area and have been asked for documentation of services you can provide in your specialty area. What documentation should you provide?

A) The scope of practice guidelines for general nursing practice in the state of which you will be practicing.

B) The scope of practice guidelines for hospice and palliative care nursing in the state of which you will practicing.

C) Treatments and procedures that have been included in your collaborative agreement and filed with your state board of nursing.

D) Your state license to practice, your board certification, your recent CEU's in hospice and palliative care nursing and specialty certificates.

111. All of the following are examples of professional development activities EXCEPT:

A) Striving to "stay under the radar" and inch toward retirement.

B) Participating in professional organizations.

C) Presenting at conferences and publishing.

D) Educating colleagues and mentoring students.

112. The National Consensus Project for Quality Palliative Care defines primary palliative care as being inclusive to all medical professionals and should focus on alleviating suffering, promoting quality of life, and using an interdisciplinary approach to care, as well as:

A) Basic symptom management, open communication, and advance directive discussions.

B) Pain management, ethics, and advance directive discussions.

C) Right to die autonomy, family cohesion and decision making, and DNR.

D) Clergy, social work, and therapies.

113. Which organization develops, disseminates, and updates the *Clinical Practice Guidelines for Quality Palliative Care?*

A) Hospice and Palliative Care Credentialing Center (HPCC).

B) National Hospice and Palliative Care Organization.

C) National Coalition for Hospice and Palliative Care.

D) American Nurses Association (ANA).

- Know the position statements for major nursing organizations.
- Know the definitions of autonomy, beneficence, non-maleficence, veracity, justice, and confidentiality.
- Know what palliative sedation is and how it fits into the scope of practice for nurse practitioners.
- Know when an ethics consult is recommended and when one is not.
- Know the qualities of effective leadership.
- Know how to effectively implement change within an organization.
- Know how to gain co-worker buy-in for policy changes.
- Know how to promote team building.
- Be familiar with preventing burn-out and examples of stress-reducing activities.
- Be knowledgeable of how to remain professionally active within your specialty.
- Know where to look up guidelines for practice for hospice and palliative care nursing.

Practice Test 4: Answers and Rationales

101. B) Check with your state's scope of practice prior to proceeding.

Feedback: Check the scope of practice for your state whenever you question the parameters of your scope and what is permissible in your state. Most patients with end-stage liver disease, requiring frequent paracentesis, have a catheter placed allowing them to self-drain at home.

102. A) A colleague starts crying at the death of a patient.

Feedback: Although showing empathy for a patient's illness is a sign of compassion, reaching heightened emotional states, such as crying or screaming, has been shown in studies to be more indicative of overwork and burnout. Although anger and irritability are signs of professional burnout, aggravation with patient choices and observing incompetence within the work environment does not necessarily indicate provider burnout. Realizing it may be time to take a vacation is a good way to prevent burnout.

103. A) Plan a retreat allowing for open discussion outside of the work environment.

Feedback: The ability to address colleagues in a non-formal, relaxed environment helps to level the playing field, and allows for a more open discussion. If colleagues feel their opinions matter and are involved in the process, they are much more likely to buy into organizational changes. The success of change implementation within an organization is more apt to fail without buy-in from those that will be affected by the desired changes. Some may even leave the organization and find employment elsewhere.

104. A) Veracity.

Feedback: Veracity is the duty to tell the truth. Beneficence is the duty to act in a way that would best benefit the patient. Non-maleficence is the duty to do no harm. Justice is fairness for all.

105. C) A patient's health record remains confidential for up to 50 years after they have died.

Feedback: The HITECH Act's modification to the HIPAA Privacy Rule, effective January 2018, grants access to a patient's personal health information (PHI) 50 years after a patient has died.

106. C) Mindfulness training.

Feedback: Mindfulness training has been shown to reduce burnout, increase empathy, and increase mood. It may not be possible to cut back work hours to part-time, and taking a vacation is only a temporary solution. Cognitive-behavioral therapy is used to change negative patterns of thought.

107. D) When a family is demanding life-sustaining treatment for an unconscious patient for their own financial benefit of keeping them alive.

Feedback: Ethical consults are not required if the patient is able to make their own health care decisions, regardless if the family agrees with their decisions or not. Conflicts within the family or differences in opinion do not render an ethics consult but render further discussion with the healthcare team. An ethical concern is when decisions are being made that are not in the patient's best interest, and the patient's quality of life continues to decline due to these decisions. This is seen when someone is benefiting financially from keeping a person alive, regardless of the circumstances and undue suffering of the patient.

108. D) Responsible behavior by the provider, since it is their license and their decision.

Feedback: In a pain clinic or other area of medicine, a provider is well within their rights not to continue to give opioids to patients that have broken their opioid contracts, or the providers feels they are abusing or misusing their prescriptions. In the arena of hospice care, where a patient should have less than 6 months to live due to a terminal illness, addressing pain and end-of-life issues are imperative. The provider should gather more information such as, "Is your pain not being controlled with your current opioid regimen?" It is also worth remembering that care is provided by a "team approach" (interdisciplinary team), and the provider is not acting alone as in the primary care environment. In hospice, many people are involved in the decisions regarding the patients plan of care. The ANA states the goal of hospice and palliative care nursing is to "promote and improve the patient's quality of life through relief of suffering along the course of the illness." If a provider feels their license is at risk, or is having ethical concerns regarding a patient's issues, they should present their concerns in a professional manner to the team or escalate the issues to a higher authority.

109. D) Deny the request because this would require respiratory therapy and hospice does not provide this type of support.

Feedback: You would not be able to deny the request, but you could fully inform the patient and family of the consequences of their decision, as well as set up a family meeting with the interdisciplinary team for further support. Increasing opioids for symptom management, and further addressing quality of life issues and advance directives, is imperative with ALS patients. The patient would have to come off of hospice care if they choose to pursue trach placement and mechanical ventilation. The family also has to realize they may not be able to care for the patient at home if this occurs, and placement for vent-dependent ALS patients is very difficult to find and extremely costly.

110. B) The scope of practice guidelines for hospice and palliative nursing, in conjunction with the practice restrictions governed by the state in which you are practicing.

Feedback: Currently, prescribing for opioids in hospice and palliative care is held to different regulatory standards than that of general practice, but state law trumps all other avenues to practice, unless you are associated with a government agency.

111. A) Striving to "stay under the radar" and inch toward retirement.

Feedback: Staying active and engaged in your profession and specialty helps keep the provider knowledgeable and demonstrates leadership strength. This is also a good way to be a role model for future providers or new providers.

112. A) Basic symptom management, open communication, and advance directive discussions.

Feedback: The NCP is composed of four large end-of-life organizations (HPNA, AAHPM, NHPCO, and CAPC), and they establish the clinical guidelines of practice to ensure quality palliative care. The NCP's definition of Palliative Care is inclusive for alleviating suffering, promoting quality of life, using an interdisciplinary approach, basic symptom management, open communication, and advance directives. All other answers are incorrect.

113. C) National Coalition for Hospice and Palliative Care

Feedback: The National Coalition for Hospice and Palliative Care developed the National Consensus Project for Quality Palliative Care. A task force was assembled for achieving quality initiatives and guidelines for practice. The National Consensus Project incorporates national organizations such as the American Academy of Hospice and Palliative Medicine, Hospice and Palliative Nurses Association, and the National Palliative Care Research Center.

Chapter 5

Systems Issues: Practice Test 5

The topic of systems issues encompasses approximately 10% of the examination. This portion of the test focuses on quality improvement, cost-effective care, barriers for receiving hospice and palliative care, Medicare regulations for hospice services, and resource utilization. Let's see how you do.

114. Choose the best definition of quality improvement:

   A) Quality Improvement is a method for continual organizational restructure for upholding accreditation standards.

   B) Quality Improvement is a division or department within organizations designed to review pitfalls or damages within an organization and provide recommendations for punitive action when necessary.

   C) Quality Improvement is a philosophy that organizations use to benchmark, reduce waste, increase efficiency, and improve outcomes using research as a means for continuous evaluation and improvement.

   D) Quality Improvement is an avenue for punishing employees for misconduct and medical errors as a way of reducing lawsuits.

115. An 82 y/o patient tells you they have had enough, and they no longer want aggressive treatment for their terminal illness. They state they just want to go home with hospice but aren't sure they can afford it. You know the patient has Medicare. You explain:

   A) Medicare Part D covers your hospice costs.

   B) You pay upfront, but Medicare will reimburse you.

   C) Medicare Part B covers your hospice costs.

D) Medicare Part A covers your hospice costs.

116. For a patient to meet hospice eligibility with the diagnosis of COPD, they must meet three criteria. What are those criteria?

A) 1. Dyspnea at rest, unresponsiveness to bronchodilators, and decreased functional capacity.

2. Progression of disease evidenced by increasing doctor visits or hospitalizations.

3. Documentation within the last 3 months of hypoxemia at rest, oxygen saturation of < 88% on room air, and hypercapnia evidenced by pCO_2 > 50mmHg.

B) 1. Dyspnea with minimal activity, limited response to bronchodilators, and a decrease in functional capacity.

2. Progression of disease evidenced by increasing doctor visits or hospitalizations.

3. Documentation within the last 3 months of hypoxemia at rest, oxygen saturation of < 78% on room air, and hypercapnia evidenced by pCO_2 > 60mmHg.

C) 1. Dyspnea with exertion, responsiveness to bronchodilators, and decreased functional capacity.

2. Progression of disease evidenced by increasing doctor visits or hospitalizations.

3. Documentation within the last 3 months of hypoxemia at rest, oxygen saturation of < 80% on room air, and hypercapnia evidenced by pCO_2 > 50mmHg.

D) 1. Dyspnea at rest, limited response to bronchodilators, and decreased functional capacity.

2. Progression of disease evidenced by increases in medications and dosages.

3. Documentation within the last 3 months of hypoxemia at rest, oxygen saturation of < 70% on room air, and hypercapnia evidenced by pCO_2 > 58mmHg.

117. When ordering a work-up on a hospice patient for controlling symptoms and addressing quality of life, the work-up should:

A) Be cost effective, minimally invasive, and in line with the patient's goals of care.

B) Should include tests that allow for a more accurate diagnosis, such as MRI's and ABGs, so the patient does not have to continually return for additional testing.

C) Be very thorough, since this is part of their hospice benefit and will be paid for by Medicare.

D) Order as much as possible so that you do not miss anything in case of a lawsuit.

118. Which statement below is part of the Hospice & Palliative Nurses Association (HPNA) position statement regarding the *Value of the Advanced Practice Nurse in Palliative Care?*

A) Prohibits nurses' participation in assisted suicide and euthanasia because these acts are in direct violation of the *Code of Ethics for Nurses with Interpretive Statements*, the ethical traditions and goals of the profession, and its covenant with society.

B) APRNs have the knowledge and clinical judgment to provide primary palliative care in all settings, including advanced care planning. They are uniquely qualified and positioned to address the multiple needs of individuals facing life-threatening, progressive illness. If used to the extent of their scope of practice, they can both improve healthcare quality and access to care.

C) Nurses must advocate for and play an active role in initiating discussions about DNRs with patients, families, and members of the health care team.

D) Adults with decision-making capacity, and surrogate decision-makers for patients who lack capacity, are in the best position to weigh the risks, benefits, and burdens of nutrition and hydration at the end of life, in collaboration with the health care team.

119. A patient is concerned that Medicare will not pay for their stay in a skilled nursing facility (SNF) when they are discharged from the hospital. You tell the patient:

A) Medicare will pay for 100 days in a SNF after a hospital discharge.

B) Medicare will pay for 120 days in a SNF after a hospital discharge.

C) Medicare will pay for 60 days in a SNF after a hospital discharge.

D) Medicare will pay for 30 days in a SNF after a hospital discharge.

120. The four levels of care included within the Medicare Hospice Benefit are:

A) 24/7 nursing care, routine hospice care, hospice travel care, and caregiver support.

B) Routine hospice care, general inpatient care, continuous homecare, and inpatient respite care.

C) Home visits by a RN, LPN, and certified nurse's aide, emergent hospital transportation and procedural care, coverage of medically necessary supplies and equipment, and physician oversight of medical needs and medication review.

D) All medications, periodic nursing care, caregiver support, and adjunct professional services such as social work, clergy, and dietitian.

121. Which level of care within the Medicare Hospice Benefit provides around-the-clock RN direct patient care for acute symptom management within a Medicare certified hospital or hospice inpatient facility?

A) Inpatient Respite Care (IRC).

B) Continuous Home Care (CHC).

C) General Inpatient Care (GIP).

D) Routine Hospice Care (RHC).

122. A patient's wife asks you how long her husband can be on hospice. You reply:

A) Under Medicare guidelines, a patient that is eligible for hospice will have one 30-day benefit period, and then an unlimited number thereafter.

B) Under Medicare guidelines, a patient that is eligible for hospice will have a 6-month benefit period, and then 30-day periods thereafter.

C) Under Medicare guidelines, a patient that is eligible for hospice will have two 90-day benefit periods, and then an unlimited number of 60-day periods thereafter.

D) Under Medicare guidelines, a patient that is eligible for hospice will have two 30-day benefit periods, and then up to four 60-day periods thereafter.

123. An issue has continued to arise at your job regarding prescribing habits and cost-effectiveness. What would be the most effective way to bring about changing provider prescribing habits and implementing new policy changes?

A) Do a literature review and hold a meeting with the evidence you have gathered and inform your colleagues of the upcoming policy changes.

B) Assemble a challenge for employees by arranging small work groups, and the group that comes up with the most effective solution wins a prize.

C) Hold a meeting regarding the new rules of what providers can order. Have employees sign a form acknowledging they have been told about the changes and the consequences that will incur if the new policy has been broken.

D) Walk around the unit and politely ask providers if they would mind ordering less expensive medications so that you do not get in trouble with upper management.

124. Which items would NOT be covered under Medicare Part B?

A) Ambulance transport and durable medical equipment.

B) Getting a second opinion and clinical research.

C) Hospice care and hospitalization.

D) Limited drug coverage.

125. When should a palliative care referral be made?

A) As soon as a diagnosis is made for a life-limiting illness.

B) When the patient is ready for hospice services.

C) When the family starts raising questions regarding the disease trajectory and treatment options.

D) When all other treatment options have been exhausted without success.

126. What is a known barrier to end-of-life care?

A) Patients living in rural areas.

B) Referrals from specialists for hospice care.

C) Lack of insurance or limited finances.

D) Families not wanting a death in their home.

127. A COPD patient will be eligible for hospice if they have all of the following EXCEPT:

A) A PO2 $\leq$ 55 mmHg at rest on room air.

B) Oxygen saturation $\leq$ 88% at rest on room air.

C) Hypercapnia evidenced by pCO2 > 50 mmHg.

D) Responds well to bronchodilators.

128. A homeless patient under hospice care for stage 4 metastatic breast cancer is living in a shelter. What type of pain medication would be most appropriate for this patient?

A) Oxycodone.
B) Hydromorphone.
C) Tramadol.
D) Methadone.

Pearls
for
Passing

- When prescribing, think of cost-efficiency and using one medication that will help with several issues, instead of prescribing a single medication for each issue. Some side effects of medications can actually replace another pill.
- Hospice used to have facilities called "hospice houses," but due to regulatory changes, these no longer exist. "Hospice houses" are now called "inpatient" short-term symptom management facilities. Remember to transfer patients to these "inpatient" facilities for symptoms that cannot be managed in the home, or when the family is in need for a respite break as per Medicare guidelines.
- Know what healthcare members must be included in an interdisciplinary team as per Medicare guidelines. For example, does Medicare require clergy to be part of the interdisciplinary team?
- Be familiar with simple, cost effective treatment options for recurring issues such as bowel obstructions in cancer patients, or paracentesis approaches for end-stage liver disease patients.
- Know what informed consent is.
- Know what agency sets the standards for quality improvement initiatives.
- Know Medicare standards for hospice care.

Practice Test 5: Answers and Rationales

114. C) Quality Improvement is a philosophy that organizations use to benchmark, reduce waste, increase efficiency, and improve outcomes using research as a means for continuous evaluation and improvement.

Feedback: Quality Improvement is not a department or a single entity, but an ongoing conglomeration of approaches for improving cost reduction, efficiency, satisfaction scores, and overall outcomes. Research-based outcomes are now the standard for implementing changes within an organization. Benchmarking against successful organizations is another tool used in quality improvement, as well as surveys, root cause analysis, and a continual re-evaluation process. Quality Improvement is not meant to be a means for punitive action. It is now encouraged to report medical errors and other mishaps as a way of preventing further events, instead of a means of punishment for an individual. An organization preparing for an accreditation visit is not a valid definition of Quality Improvement.

115. D) Medicare Part A covers your hospice benefit.

Feedback: You are eligible for hospice care if you have Medicare Part A and have a prognosis of 6 months or less. Medicare Part B covers medically necessary services to diagnose and treat a medical condition, as well as preventive services. Medicare Part D is for prescription drug coverage.

116. A) 1. Dyspnea at rest, unresponsiveness to bronchodilators, and decreased functional capacity.

2. Progression of disease evidenced by increasing doctor visits or hospitalizations.

3. Documentation within the last 3 months of hypoxemia at rest, oxygen saturation of < 88% on room air, and hypercapnia evidenced by pCO2 > 50mmHg.

Feedback: For patients to meet hospice criteria with COPD they must have severe lung disease with documentation supporting:

1. Dyspnea at rest, unresponsiveness to bronchodilators, and decreased functional capacity (ie: bed to chair with fatigue and cough).

2. Progression of disease evidenced by increasing doctor visits or hospitalizations.

3. Documentation within the last 3 months of hypoxemia at rest, oxygen saturation of < 88% on

room air, and hypercapnia evidenced by $pCO_2 > 50mmHg$. Typically, ABGs are not drawn in the home, but a $pO_2 <55mmHg$ by ABG also meets criteria.

117. A) Be cost effective, minimally invasive, and in line with the patient's goals of care.

Feedback: Medicare is very particular as to what is covered under hospice care. The patient's prognosis must be 6 months or less to live. Focus is not on heroic intervention or expensive testing for simple symptom management. Also, keep the goals of care in mind when considering orders, and continue to discuss the patient's case at interdisciplinary meetings.

118. B) APRNs have the knowledge and clinical judgment to provide primary palliative care in all settings including advanced care planning. They are uniquely qualified and positioned to address the multiple needs of individuals facing life-threatening, progressive illness. If used in the scope of their practice, they can both improve healthcare quality and access to care.

Feedback: Part of the HPNA position statement includes the fact that APRNs have the knowledge and clinical judgment to provide primary palliative care in all settings, including advanced care planning. The other position statements are from the ANA regarding Euthanasia, Assisted Suicide, Aid in Dying, and Nutrition and Hydration at the End of Life.

119. A) Medicare will pay for 100 days in a SNF after a hospital discharge.

Feedback: Medicare will pay for up to 100 days for skilled nursing care provided in a skilled nursing facility (SNF), post-hospitalization. The other answers are not correct.

120. B) Routine hospice care, general inpatient care, continuous home care, and inpatient respite care.

Feedback: The four levels of care under the Medicare Hospice Benefit are Routine Hospice Care (RHC), General Inpatient Care (GIP), Continuous Home Care (CHC), and Inpatient Respite Care (IRC). Each level of care has a different reimbursement rate. The other answers are not reflective of the four levels of the Medicare Hospice Benefit, although some answers can be incorporated into a specific level of care. Appropriate documentation must support the level of care a patient is receiving or reimbursement will be denied.

121. C) General Inpatient Care (GIP).

Feedback: General Inpatient Care (GIP) is provided for acute symptom management that cannot be adequately controlled in the home or other environments. Approved GIP settings include Medicare certified hospitals, and hospice inpatient facilities that afford 24-hour RN direct patient care services. The other levels of care do not reflect acute symptom management and 24-hour direct RN support in a hospital or hospice inpatient facility.

122. C) Under Medicare guidelines, a patient that is eligible for hospice will have two 90-day benefit periods and then an unlimited number of 60-day periods thereafter.

Feedback: The Medicare Hospice Benefit is composed of two 90-day periods, and then an unlimited number of subsequent 60-day periods. A certification for terminal illness must be obtained during the first 90-day period. Face-to-face visits must be made with the patient by a nurse practitioner or physician prior to recertification for each benefit period. The other answers do not reflect accurate Medicare guidelines.

123. B) Assemble a challenge for employees by arranging small work groups, and the group that comes up with the most effective solution wins a prize.

Feedback: By allowing employee engagement and involvement in the change process will increase the likelihood of successful implementation. Having a dictator, authoritarian type of leadership style, and mandating rules with punitive treatment if not followed, has been associated with higher employee attrition rates and poorer outcomes. Studies show under a dictator type of leadership style, the changes are only adhered to when the "dictator" is around; otherwise, the changes are ineffective. On the other hand, the less assertive, laissez-faire type of leadership style have shown to have ineffective outcomes as well.

124. C) Hospice care and hospitalization.

Feedback: Medicare Part B covers two types of services: medically necessary services and preventive services. This includes supplies, healthcare to prevent illness, clinical research, ambulance services, DME, mental health care, receiving a second opinion before surgery, and limited outpatient drug coverage. Medicare Part A covers hospitalizations, hospice care, home health services, nursing home care, and skilled nursing facility (SNF) care.

125. A) As soon as a diagnosis is made for a life-limiting illness.

Feedback: Studies have found the sooner a patient is referred to palliative care, the sooner improvements in quality of life are seen, hospitalizations are decreased, symptoms are better controlled, and the patient is more willing to have hospice services at the end-of-life. The patient can be on palliative care while receiving life-sustaining treatment.

126. A) Patients living in rural areas.

Feedback: Patients living in rural areas are less likely to receive hospice care due to the limited number of hospice organizations located in rural areas, as opposed to the more populated urban areas. Patients that do not have insurance or have limited finances can most likely qualify for Medicaid or other government-funded programs. Although the term "hospice house" is no longer used, patients that are imminently dying can be transferred to an inpatient facility for symptom management and alleviating the family's fears of the patient dying in their home.

127. D) Responds well to bronchodilators.

Feedback: For eligibility to hospice for pulmonary disease, the patient must have at least three indicators. The patient must exhibit dyspnea at rest, little or no response to bronchodilators, or decreased functional capacity, AND evidence of disease progression such as increased ER visits or hospitalizations, AND documentation within the past 3 months of $pO2 < 55$ mmHg at rest on room air, oxygen saturation <88%, or hypercapnia evidenced by $pCO2 > 50$ mmHg. Patients that are still responding to bronchodilators are most likely not ready for hospice care.

128. D) Methadone.

Feedback: Due to the high probability of this patient's medication being stolen, it is wise to prescribe a medication with little street value, such as methadone. Hydromorphone (Dilaudid) is one of the leading drugs used for diversion, and street prices range from $5 to $100 a tablet. Oxycodone is typically priced at $1 per mg, so a provider writing for Percocet 10/325 TID #90 will have a street value of $900. Methadone has a very low street value and therefore would be the best medication to prescribe for vulnerable patient populations such as those living in homeless shelters. Tramadol is a poor choice because it most likely would not be strong enough to adequately control her pain.

Chapter 6

Medication Review

Opioids are a necessity in hospice care. A common fear of patients when dying is not the fear of the unknown, like most would think, but instead it is not wanting to die in pain. Being able to allow patients to make the transition as comfortably as possible is one of the most valued aspects of hospice.

The chapters to follow will start by first reviewing the most commonly used drugs in the hospice environment. The medication review will include common drug ranges for each drug, and what the drugs are typically used for in hospice care. This book will also cover the drug hierarchy, as to what to start with and what to prescribe next when a drug loses efficacy, as well opioid conversions. Hospice care has typically used the same drugs for many years, and not many newer synthetic versions have been added.

One of the most frequently asked questions is, "What is the maximum dosage for opioids?" In theory, opioid doses can be continually titrated upwards in accordance with a patient's tolerance. There is no maximum dosage for opioids. A Cochrane review of 62 pain management studies in cancer patients showed an average daily dose of 100-250mg of morphine, with a range between 25-2000mg. Some institutions have a maximum dosage of morphine set at 6000mg a day for cancer patients, although most clinicians will typically try other methods of pain relief before going this high.

One way to monitor dosage amounts, and how much the patient typically needs of a medication, is to give prn orders for the same drug that you are starting. This will allow for additional coverage if the dose you have started is not effective enough and will also give you a review of how many prn doses are being needed. You can then adjust the medication for better coverage. When you see that a patient needs frequent immediate release medications, it is easier to switch them to extended release with prn immediate release for additional coverage. The recommendation for dosing breakthrough, or as needed medication, is 10% to 15% of the daily long-acting dose. Another thing to monitor is "end-dose-failure" of extended release opioids. This occurs when the medication stops working for the patient sooner than expected. This can be evidenced by the need for prn medications toward the end of the extended-release dosing. If this occurs, you can increase the dosage of the extended release medication or schedule every eight hours instead of every twelve.

Patient Controlled Analgesia (PCA) is also commonly used in hospice. The two most commonly used medications for PCA are morphine and hydromorphone (Dilaudid). A chapter is designated to starting a PCA, changing a patient to a PCA, how to discontinue a PCA and switch to oral medication, and how to maintain a PCA for optimal symptom management. Remember, when ordering medication for a PCA, it is best to use a 10:1 ratio instead of a 1:1 ratio, or the bag will be used very quickly, and pharmacy will have to continually send more.

Another consideration is the use of a Macy catheter for drug administration. A Macy catheter looks very similar to a Foley catheter, except it is placed in the rectum. The following is a list of medications that can be given via a Macy catheter:

Acetaminophen	Lorazepam (Ativan)
Alprazolam IR (Xanax)	Metoclopramide (Reglan)
Chlorpramazine (Thorazine)	Odansetron (Zofran)
Clonazepam (Klonopin)	Opioids IR
Dexamethasone (Decadron)	Phenobarbital
Diazepam (Valium)	Prochlorperazine (Compazine)
Haloperidol (Haldol)	Promethazine (Phenergan)

Other considerations include the sublingual (SL) route for giving medications as well as having to crush medications.

Commonly used medications that can be crushed include:

Acetaminophen	Lorazepam (Ativan)
Alprazolam IR(Xanax)	Metocipramide (Reglan)
Chlorpromazine (Thorazine)	Ondansetron (Zofran)
Clonazepam (Klonopin)	Opioids IR
Dexamethsone (Decadron)	Phenobarbital
Diazepam (Valium)	Phenytoin IR (Dilantin)
Glycopyrrolate (Robinul)	Prochlorperazine (Compazine)
Haloperidol (Haldol)	Promethazine (Phenergan)

Commonly used medications that can be given SL include:

Alprazolam (Xanax)	Lorazepam (Ativan)
Chlorpromazine (Thorazine)	Metoclopramine (Reglan)
Clonazepam (Klonopin)	Ondansetron (Zofran)
Diazepam (Valium)	Opioids IR
Haloperidol (Haldol)	Phenobarbital

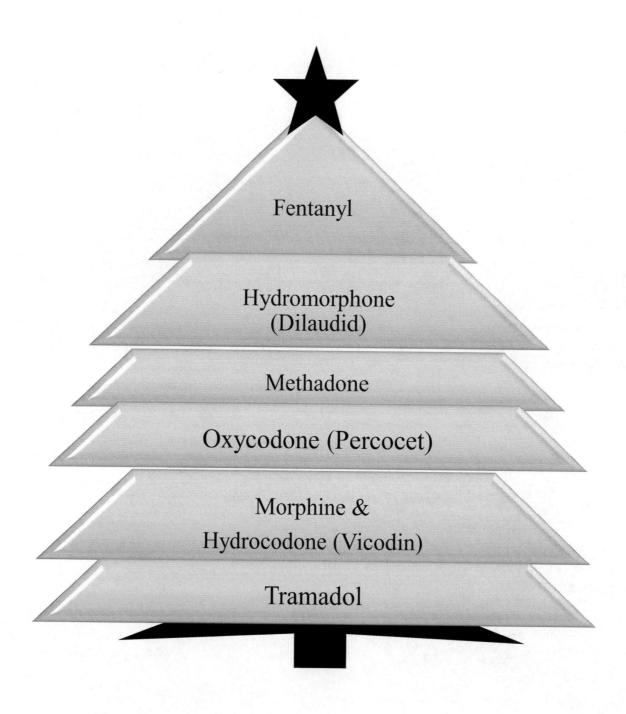

From weakest to strongest

Many hospices have an order set used for hospice admissions. These are good to have because it reminds the clinician of typical medications that are needed for hospice patients and gives a starting point for drug administration.

Example of Hospice Order Set

ANXIETY Lorazepam (Ativan) ☐ 0.5 mg tab – 1 tab PO/SL Q4H prn mild anxiety. ☐ 1 mg tab – 1 tab PO/SL Q4H prn moderate anxiety. Phenobarbital ☐ 64.8 mg – PO/IM/IV TID ☐ 129.6 mg – PO/IM/IV TID for severe anxiety	**NAUSEA/VOMITTING** Prochlorperazine (Compazine) ☐ 10mg tab – 1tab Q6H prn ☐ 25mg supp – 1 supp pr Q12H prn ☐ Odansetron (Zofran) ODT ☐ 4mg tab – 1 tab PO/SL every 6 hours prn (Max 24mg per 24 hours).
RESTLESSNESS Haloperidol ☐ 1mg tab – 1 tab PO/SL Q4H prn ☐ 5mg/ml inj – 2mg IM Q2H prn severe restlessness Seroquel (Quetiapine) - Consider for ATC coverage ☐ 25mg tab PO QHS	**PAIN/DYSPNEA** Morphine Concentrate (Roxanol) Oral Solution 20mg.ml ☐ 5mg/0.25ml – PO/SL Q4H prn pain 1-3 (30MG/24H) ☐ 10mg/0.5ml – PO/SL Q4H prn pain 4-6 (60MG/24H) ☐ 20mg/1 ml – PO/SL Q4H prn pain 7-10 (120MG/24H) Oxycodone (If allergic to Morphine) *MAY CRUSH TABS AND MIX WITH 2-5ML OF H2O FOR SL ADMINISTRATION* ☐ 5mg PO/SL Q4H prn pain 1-3 ☐ 10mg PO/SL Q4H prn pain 4-6 ☐ 20mg PO/SL/Q4H prn pain 7-10 Acetaminophen (Tylenol) 325mg tabs Max 3 gm/24H ☐ 2 tabs PO Q4H prn pain ☐ 1 supp (650mg) PR Q4H prn
DIARRHEA Diphenoxylate 2.5mg/Atropine 0.025mg (Lomotil) ☐ 2 tabs po x1 then 1 after LBM prn	
INSOMNIA ☐ Temazepam (Restoril) – 15mg po QHS prn ☐ Risperidone (Risperdal) 0.25 - 0.5mg po QHS	
CHEST CONGESTION ☐ NACL 0.9% NEB -Administer 3ml via nebulizer every 2 hours prn	**BOWEL REGIMEN** Senna/docusate (Senokot-S) ☐ 1 tab po bid
CANDIDIASIS	☐ 2 tabs po bid Bisacodyl (Dulcolax) Suppository

☐ Nystatin SUSP 100,000 units per mL – 4ml PO QID x7 days. Swish in mouth for as long as possible. May swallow or spit.	☐ 10mg supp PR daily prn constipation May repeat x1 in 6 hours if no results
EXCESSIVE SECRETIONS (first try repositioning) Hyoscyamine Sulfate (Levsin) ☐ 0.125mg – 1 tab SL q6h prn mild to mod ☐ 0.125mg – 2 tabs SL q6h prn severe Robinul (glycopyrrolate) ☐ 0.2 mg SC Q6H prn Scopalamine Patch ☐ 1mg - Apply one patch Q72H	**ADJUNCT MEDICATIONS** ☐ Decadron 4mg PO/SL @ 0800 and 1400 – May give first dose now. ☐ DuoNeb 2.5/0.5mg per 3ml Q6H ATC while awake. ☐ Nystatin Topical Powder 100,000 units per gram - apply to affected area TID until resolved.

Common Medications

Some of the most commonly used medications in hospice are listed on the following pages. The typical drug ranges are listed for each drug, but these drug ranges often go beyond what is considered standard due to drug tolerances, patient body size, or intractable symptoms that are difficult to manage. Once you become comfortable with using these drugs, you will know what to take into consideration when starting a new drug. For example, if you have a 250-pound man that has taken medications in the past, you would typically not start him on a "starting dose" of a new drug. Chances are it will not do much for him and you will be receiving a call stating as such very soon.

Generic Name	Indication	Available Dose Forms	Standard Adult Dosing	Maximum Dose
Acetaminophen	Pain, Fever	Tab: 325mg/500mg Supp: 650mg	650mg PO Q4H prn	4g/day
Albuterol/ Ipratropium	Beta Adrenergic Agonists- Anticholinergic	Inhal: Sol:3-0.5mg/3mL	3mL NEB QID prn	6 doses/ day
Alprazolam	Anxiety	Tab: 0.25, 0.5,1,2mg ER Tabs: 0.5,2,2,3mg Sol(PO): 1mg per mL	0.25-0.5mg PO tid	4mg/day
Baclofen	Muscle spasms	Tab: 5mg;10mg;20mg	20-80 mg/day PO tid-qid	80mg/day
Benzonatate	Cough	Cap: 100mg	100-200mg PO tid prn	600mg/day
Bisacodyl	Constipation	Tab: 5mg Supp: 10mg	5-15mg PO QID prn	30mg/day
Bumetanide	Edema	Tab: 0.5mg; 1mg; 2mg IV; 0.25mg	0.5-10mg / day PO/IM/IV QD-BID	10mg/day
Diazepam	Anxiety' Restlessness	Tab: 2mg,5mg, 10mg Sol(PO): 5mg/5mL;5mg/mL Inj: 5mg/mL	2-10mg PO bid-qid	None
Fentanyl	Pain	IV:50 mcg per m/L Patch: 12,25,37.5,50,62.5 75,87.5,100mg per hour	50-100mcg IV/IM Q1-2h prn	None
Furosemide	Edema	Tab:20mg;40mg;80mg IV:10mg/mL	40-120mg/day PO QD-BID	600mg/day
Gabapentin	Neuropathic	CAP: 100mg;300mg;400mg Tab: 600mg;800mg Sol(PO): 50mg per mL	300-1200mg PO tid	3600mg/day
Glycopyrrolate	Anticholinergic	Tab: 1mg;2mg IV: 0.2mg/mL	1-2 mg PO BID-TID prn	8mg/day
Haloperidol	Agitation	Tab: 0.5,1,2,5,10,20mg Sol: 2mg/mL IV/SC: 5mg/mL	0.5-10mg PO Q1-4h	100mg/day
Hydrocodone-Acetaminophen	Pain	Tab: 5-325mg;7.5-325mg; 10-325mg Sol: 7.5-325mg/15mL	1-2 tabs -PO Q4-6h prn	1g/4h and 4g/day
Hydromorphone	Pain	Tab:2mg;4mg,8mg ER Tab:8mg,12mg,16mg, 32mg Sol (PO):1mg/mL Supp: 3mg IV: 1mg/mL;2mg/mL;10mg/mL	2-4mg IR PO Q4-6H prn sol (PO)-2.5-10mg PO Q3-6H Prn 1-4mg SC/IM/IV-Q3-6H prn Rectal-	None

			3mg PR Q6-8H prn PCA-0.05-0.4 mg IV Q6-20min. Basal rate Up to 0.5mg/h	
Hyoscyamine	Anticholinergic -Increased secretions	Tab (PO/SL): 0.125mg ER Tab: 0.375mg; Sol (PO/SL): 0.125mg/mL Elix 0.125mg/5 mL	0.125-0.25mg PO/SL Q4H prn	1.5mg/day
Ibuprofen	Pain, inflammation	Tab:100,200;400;600; 800mg Susp:20mg/mL;40mg/mL	300-800mg PO tid-qid Prn	3200mg/day
Levetiracetam	Seizures	Tab:250,500,750,100mg Sol (PO): 100mg/mL IV: 100mg/mL	500-1500mg PO/IV - q12h.	3000mg/day
Lidocaine Oropharyngeal -Viscous Solution	Pain	Sol (PO):2% 20mg/mL	4.5mg/kg Q3h prn; Gargle; May split or swallow.	4.5mg/kg Dose Up to 300mg/dose, 8 doses / 24h
Lidocaine Patch	Pain	Transdermal Patch: 5%	1 Patch Q12h prn	3 patches, x12h/day
Lorazepam	Anxiety, Restlessness	Tab: 0.5mg;1mg;2mg Sol (PO): 2mg/mL IV: 2mg/mL,4mg/mL	2-6mg/day PO/IM/IV Bid-tid	10mg/day
Methadone	Pain	Tab:5mg;10mg Sol(PO):5mg/5mL;10mg/mL Inj: 10mg/mL	40mg/day	30mg/initial Dose, 40mg On Day 1.
Morphine	Pain	IR Tab: 15mg;30mg ER Tab: -15,30,60,100,200mg Sol(PO):10mg/5mL;20mg/5mL; 100mg/5mL IV: 4mg/mL;8mg/mL;25mg/mL; 50mg/mL	2.5-10mg SC/IM/IV Q2-6h prn. PCA-0.5-2.5mg IV Q6-20min Prn Basal Rate up to 2mg/hour	None
Ondansetron	Nausea-Vomiting	Tab:4mg,8mg,16,24mg Sol(PO): 4mg/5mL IV: 2mg/mL	8mg PO/IV Q8h prn	Hepatic max 8mg/24hour
Oxycodone IR	Pain	Tab:5,10,15,20,30mg	Start 5-	None

		Sol(PO): 5mg/5mL,100mg/5mL	15mg PO Q4-6h prn	
Oxycodone ER	Pain	Tab:10,20,40,80mg.	Start 10mg ER PO Q12 hour	None
Oxycodone-Acetaminophen	Pain	Tab:2.5-325mg, 5-325mg, 7.5-325mg, 10-325mg Sol(PO):5-325mg/5mL	2.5-10mg PO q6h Prn	1g/4h and 4g/day
Phenobarbital	Agitation	Tab:15,16.2,30,32.4,60,64.8 97.2,100mg Sol (PO): 20mg per 5mL Inj:30mg/mL,60mg/mL,65mg/mL, 130mg/mL	30-120mg / day BID-TID	400mg/day
Promethazine	Nausea-Vomiting	Tab: 12.5mg,25mg IV: 25mg/mL, 50mg/mL Supp: 12.5mg, 25mg	12.5-25mg PO/IM/IV Q4-6h Prn	100mg/day
Quetiapine IR	Agitation	Tab: 25,50,100,200,300,400mg ER Tab: 50,150,200,300,400mg	IR 150-750mg/day PO bid-tid ER 400-800mg QHS	800mg/day
Temazepam	Insomnia	Cap: 7.5mg, 15mg, 22.5mg, 30mg	7.5-30mg PO QHS	None
Tramadol	Pain	Tab: 50mg ER Tab: 100mg,200mg, 300mg	50-100 PO q4-6h Prn ER 100 – 300mg PO QD	400mg / day ER 300mg/day

Opioid Conversion:
All Things Equal to Morphine

The terms opioid rotation and opioid conversion are interchangeable. Some people say switching or substituting, but in general, you are just changing the medication or route. Opioids are changed for several reasons, such as switching to a stronger opioid for better pain control or to a weaker opioid when stronger doses are no longer needed. Opioids are also changed from PO to IV, IV to PO, PO/IV to PCA, and vice versa. Many things need to be considered when choosing a different opioid or route due to differences in potency, onset, and the half-life of the drug. Other things to consider are the patient's age, metabolic state, organ failure, costs, and available routes for giving the medication. Fortunately, there is good news. There are not many opioids and there are standard equations for conversion. There are now apps that can do all of the work for you, but it is always good to know how to convert a patient from one opioid to another, or just being able to double check that the new amount is correct. Some acronyms that are commonly used when dealing with opioids are:

- Around the clock (ATC)

- As needed/ pro re nata (PRN)

- Breakthrough dose/rescue dose (BTD)

- By mouth/orally/ per os (PO)

- Equianalgesic dose ration (EDR)

- Extended release/sustained release/long acting (ER)

- Immediate release/short acting (IR)

- Total daily dose (TDD)

There are two ways of doing the math for opioid conversion. You can use a formula that incorporates ratios, or you can use a formula of cross-multiplication. Each way will be reviewed, and you can choose which way you prefer, but both ways start by converting whatever the patient is on to morphine and totaling up their daily dose. After you have completed the math and have your new dosage for your new medication, you then have to individualize the new dose. Individualizing the new dose is important due to the phenomena of cross-tolerance and incomplete cross-tolerance. The phenomena of cross-tolerance is when a person has been on a certain drug for a long enough time that their tolerance level to that drug increases and the person will need more of the drug in order for it to become effective. Because some drugs work on the same receptors, a person can have a tolerance to a new drug they have never taken. Unfortunately, there is no way of knowing if the person has developed this tolerance, and an incomplete cross-tolerance could occur. This can lead to a greater than anticipated potency of the new drug. For this reason, you may want to consider reducing your new drug dosage by 25 to 50%. There are times when you would not do this, such as when the patient is in intractable pain, but when simply changing drugs due to an increase in prn medications for breakthrough pain, it is good practice to take incomplete cross-tolerance into consideration. When switching to methadone, the dose reduction window should be 75% to 90%, because of higher-than-anticipated potency when switching to methadone. Methadone will be reviewed separately due to its unique qualities and extensive half-life.

Rule: When changing from one opioid to another, always convert to morphine first.

The 7 most commonly used opioids are morphine, fentanyl, hydrocodone, hydromorphone, oxycodone, methadone, and tramadol. Oxycodone, hydrocodone, and tramadol are only given PO. Morphine is the most commonly used out of all of the opioids and comes in numerous forms and brands. Let's start by reviewing morphine.

MS Contin, Contin is short for continuous, and is used for ATC pain management – not prn. Since MS Contin is extended release morphine; you cannot crush or use the pill in any other way except taking it whole. Its half-life is 2-4 hours.

Roxanol is morphine oral concentrate and comes in 20mg per 1 mL. Roxanol is primarily used for patients who can no longer swallow. Roxanol can be given PO or sublingual. It is absorbed well through the mucus membranes. It has a half-life of 2 to 3 hours.

Morphine immediate release (IR) is given to patients for acute pain or for breakthrough pain. **Morphine extended release (ER)** is used for patients with chronic pain.

Oxycontin is a long acting morphine for ATC treatment of chronic pain. Half-life is 4.5 hours.

As mentioned above, one of the ways to calculate opioid conversion is by ratios. Since you want to convert everything to morphine, the ratios are between morphine and other opioids.

PO to PO Equivalents

Morphine 1mg PO = Codeine 10mg PO

Morphine 15mg PO = Codeine 150mg PO

Morphine 1mg PO = Hydrocodone (Vicodin) 1mg PO

Morphine 15mg PO = Hydrocodone (Vicodin) 15mg PO

Morphine 3mg PO = Oxycodone 2mg PO

Morphine 15mg PO = Oxycodone 10mg PO

Morphine 30mg PO = Oxycodone 20mg PO

Oxycodone is 1.5 times stronger than morphine.

Morphine 3mg PO = 1mg PO Methadone

Morphine 15mg PO = 5mg PO Methadone

Morphine 30mg PO = 10mg PO Methadone

Morphine 4mg PO = 1mg PO Hydromorphone (Dilaudid)

Morphine 15mg PO = 3.8mg PO Hydromorphone (Dilaudid)

Morphine 30mg PO = 7.5mg PO Hydromorphone (Dilaudid)

Morphine 1mg/hr IV = 25mcg/hr of transdermal Fentanyl (Patch)

24-hour PO morphine (mg)	Fentanyl Patch (mcg/hour)
30	12
60	25
120	50
180	75
240	100

PO to IV Equivalents

Morphine 3mg PO = 1 mg IV Morphine

Morphine 15mg PO = 5mg IV Morphine

Morphine 20mg PO = 1mg IV/SC/IM Hydromorphone (Dilaudid)

IV to IV Equivalents

Morphine 20mg IV = 1mg IV Hydromorphone (Dilaudid)

Morphine 10mg IV = 0.1mg IV Fentanyl

Morphine 100mg IV = 1mg IV Fentanyl

Using Ratios for Opioid Conversion

Let's try a case study to practice opioid conversion using ratios. Mary is a 64-year-old female with stage 4 lung cancer and is currently on oxycodone 40mg every 8 hours. She is having uncontrolled pain and it has been decided that she will be changed to IV hydromorphone.

Step 1

First, determine how many milligrams she is taking of her current drug in 24 hours. We know she is taking 40mg, 3x a day. 40 x 3 = **120mg**, which is the total amount of oxycodone she is currently taking in 24 hours or total daily dose (TDD).

Step 2

We now want to convert this dose to morphine. Oral oxycodone is 1.5 times more potent than oral morphine. Take the total 24-hour dose of oxycodone, which was 120mg, and multiply it by 1.5. 120mg x 1.5 = **180mg of oral morphine.** The chart below shows morphine equivalents.

24-hour Dose of Current Opioid	Conversion Ratio to PO Morphine	Equivalent Dose of PO Morphine
60mg of IV Morphine	IV morphine is 3x as potent as PO Morphine	180 milligrams oral Morphine (60x3=180)
120mg of PO Oxycodone	PO Oxycodone is roughly 1.5x more potent than PO Morphine	180 milligrams oral Morphine (120x1.5=180)
45mg of PO Hydromorphone	PO Hydromorphone is 4-7x as potent as PO Morphine	180 milligrams oral Morphine (45x4=180)
9mg of IV Hydromorphone	IV Hydromorphone is 20x as potent as PO Morphine	180 milligrams oral Morphine (9x20=180)
45mg of Oral Hydrocodone	PO Hydromorphone is roughly 4-7x as potent as oral Morphine	180 milligrams oral Morphine (45x4=180)
Transdermal fentanyl 1800 micrograms (1.8 milligrams) over 24 hours. Therefore, hourly dose is 75 mcg/hour.	Transdermal fentanyl is 100x as potent as oral Morphine	180 milligrams oral Morphine (1.8x100=180)

Step 3

Convert the 24-hour dose of oral morphine to the 24-hour equivalent of the new drug. Parenteral hydromorphone is 20 times stronger than oral morphine. Take the 180mg of oral morphine and divide it by 20mg of parenteral hydromorphone. 180/20=9mg of parenteral hydromorphone.

Step 4

Convert 9mg in 24 hours into desired frequency such as BID, TID or hourly for PCA.

Practice Question #1

Mr. Morgan has stage 4 lung cancer and is currently on MS Contin 60mg twice a day. MS Contin is simply long-acting morphine. His pain is uncontrolled, and he is being switched to oxycodone.

Now let's do an opioid conversion using a standard formula:

$$\frac{\text{Equianalgesic dose \& route for current medication (EDR)}}{\text{24 hour dose (TDD) of current drug (basal and bolus)}} = \frac{\text{Equianalgesic dose \& route for new medication (EDR)}}{\text{TDD New Opioid}}$$

Step 1

Set up the equation finding the morphine equivalent. MS Contin (morphine) 30mg PO is equivalent to Oxycodone 20mg PO.

104

Drug	IV (MG)	PO (MG)	
Morphine	10	30	←
Fentanyl	0.1	n/a	
Hydrocodone	n/a	30	
Hydromorphone	1.5	7.5	
Oxycodone	n/a	20	←
Oxymorphone	1	10	
Tramadol	n/a	120	

<u>30mg PO Morphine (EDR)</u> = <u>20mg PO Oxycodone (EDR)</u>

Step 2

The patient is currently on MS Contin (morphine) 60mg 2x a day, 60 X 2 = 120mg. The patient is on 120mg of MS Contin in 24-hours which is his total daily dose (TDD). Now plug this into your formula.

$$\frac{\text{30mg PO Morphine (EDR)}}{\textbf{120mg PO Morphine (TDD)}} = \frac{\text{20mg PO Oxycodone (EDR)}}{\underline{\hspace{4cm}}}$$

Step 3

To find the 24-hour dosage of the new medication, **you now must cross-multiply** i.e.: 120 X 20 = 2400.

$$\frac{\textbf{30mg PO Morphine (EDR)}}{\textbf{120mg PO Morphine (TDD)}} = \frac{\textbf{20mg PO Oxycodone (EDR)}}{\textbf{? mg PO Oxycodone in 24 Hours (TDD).}}$$

**** **Cross multiply 120mg x 20mg = 2400mg**

Step 4

Complete your cross multiplication:

2400mg / 30mg = 80mg in 24 hours.

Divide 80mg / 2 (for Q12H dosing) = 40mg every 12 hours.

Consider reduction for incomplete cross tolerance.

Practice Question #2

Jim is on PCA hydromorphone (Dilaudid) with a basal rate of 0.5mg / hr. and a bolus dose of 0.25mg every 10 minutes. Jim is getting ready to go home and will be switched to oral morphine.

Step 1

Set up the equation finding the morphine equivalent. IV Hydromorphone 1.5mg is equivalent to 30mg PO morphine.

Drug	IV (MG)	PO (MG)
Morphine	10	30
Fentanyl	0.1	n/a
Hydrocodone	n/a	30
Hydromorphone	1.5	7.5
Oxycodone	n/a	20
Oxymorphone	1	10
Tramadol	n/a	120

(Current)		(New)
IV Hydromorphone (Dilaudid) 1.5mg (EDR)	=	PO Morphine 30mg (EDR)
_____		_____

Step 2

The patient is currently on Hydromorphone IV 0.5mg / hr., (0.5 X 24 = 12mg) and a bolus dose of 0.25mg every 10 minutes, (0.25 X 6 = 1.5mg / hr. 1.5 mg X 24hr.= 36mg). 12 + 36 = 48mg TDD. Now plug in 48mg total daily dose (TDD) into the formula.

(Current)		**(New)**
IV Hydromorphone (Dilaudid) 1.5mg (EDR)	=	PO Morphine 30mg (EDR)

48mg Hydromorphone (Dilaudid)

Step 3

To find the 24-hour dosage of the new medication, <u>**you now must cross-multiply**</u> i.e.:

** Cross Multiply 48x30=1440.

(Current)		**(New)**
IV Hydromorphone (Dilaudid) 1.5mg (EDR)	=	PO Morphine **30mg** (EDR)
48 mg Hydromorphone (Dilaudid		? mg Morphine over 24-hours (TDD) **48 x 30= 1440**

Step 4

Complete your cross multiplication:

1440mg divided by 1.5mg = 960mg

Reduce by 25% for incomplete cross tolerance

(960 X 0 .75) = 720mg

Divide dose by 3 for every 8-hour dosing

720 / 3 = 240mg every 8 hours.

Practice Question #3

Jennifer is on morphine ER 30mg PO every 12 hours and morphine IR 15mg PO every 4 hours prn for breakthrough pain. She is now being started on PCA hydromorphone (Dilaudid). Calculate the new basal and bolus rate for the Dilaudid PCA.

Step 1

Set up the equation finding the morphine equivalent. IV Hydromorphone 1.5mg is equivalent to 30mg PO morphine.

Drug	IV (MG)	PO (MG)
Morphine	10	30 ←
Fentanyl	0.1	n/a
Hydrocodone	n/a	30
Hydromorphone	1.5 ←	7.5
Oxycodone	n/a	20
Oxymorphone	1	10
Tramadol	n/a	120

$$\frac{\text{PO Morphine } 30mg \text{ (EDR)}}{} = \frac{\text{IV Hydromorphone (Dilaudid) } 1.5mg \text{ (EDR)}}{}$$

Step 2

The patient is currently on morphine ER 30mg PO every 12 hours and morphine IR 15mg PO every 4 hours prn. Calculate the total amount of morphine the patient is on in 24 hours.

Morphine ER 30mg X 2 = 60mg and Morphine IR 15mg X 6 = 90mg

60mg + 90mg = **150mg (TDD)**

Step 3

To find the 24-hour dosage of the new medication, you now must cross-multiply i.e.:

Cross Multiply   150 X 1.5 = 225 mg

$$\frac{\text{PO Morphine } 30\text{mg (EDR)}}{\textbf{150mg PO morphine (TDD)}} = \frac{\text{IV Hydromorphone (Dilaudid) } \textbf{1.5mg (EDR)}}{\text{Cross multiple 150mg x 1.5} = \textbf{225mg}}$$

Step 4

Complete your cross multiplication:

Divide 225mg by 30mg (225/30) = 7.5mg

Reduce by 25% for incomplete cross tolerance

7.5mg X 0.75 = 5.6 mg

5.6 mg / 24 = 0.23 mg

Hydromorphone (Dilaudid) dose is 0.23 mg / hr. basal rate

Reduce basal rate by 50% for bolus which would be

0.23/2 OR 0.23 X 0.50 = 0.115 round to 0.12

0.12 mg every 10 minutes.

Practice Question #4

Don is on Morphine ER 60mg PO BID and MSIR 30mg every 4 hours prn breakthrough pain.

He is being switched to Fentanyl PCA. Calculate his bolus and basal rates.

Step 1

Set up the equation finding the morphine equivalent. Morphine 30mg PO is equivalent to

IV Fentanyl 0.1mg.

Drug	IV (MG)	PO (MG)
Morphine	10	30 ←
Fentanyl	0.1 ←	n/a
Hydrocodone	n/a	30
Hydromorphone	1.5	7.5
Oxycodone	n/a	20
Oxymorphone	1	10
Tramadol	n/a	120

$$\frac{30\text{mg PO Morphine (EDR)}}{\underline{\hspace{4cm}}} = \frac{0.1\text{mg IV Fentanyl (EDR)}}{\underline{\hspace{4cm}}}$$

Step 2

The patient is currently on morphine ER 60mg PO twice a day and MSIR 30mg every 4 hours

as needed. Calculate the total amount of morphine the patient is on in 24 hours.

60mg X 2 = **120mg** and 30mg X 6 = **180mg**

120mg + 180mg = **300mg TDD**

The patient is on a total of 300mg of morphine a day.

Step 3

To find the 24-hour dosage of the new medication, **you now must cross-multiply**

ie: Cross Multiply   300 X 0.1 = 30

$$\frac{\text{30mg PO Morphine (EDR)}}{\textbf{300mg PO Morphine (TDD)}} = \frac{\textbf{0.1mg IV Fentanyl (EDR)}}{\text{Cross multiple}}$$

300mg X 0.1mg = **30mg**

Step 4

Complete your cross multiplication:

30mg divided by 30mg = 1mg

Reduce by 25% for incomplete cross intolerance

1mg x 0.75 = 0.75mg

Divide 0.75mg by 24 hours for an hourly rate

0.75mg / 24 = 0.031mg

Convert 0.031mg to mcg by

Move the decimal over 3 places to the right = 31mcg/hr.

Bolus is 50% of basal rate

31 divided by 2 = 15.5mcg every 10 minutes.

**Note

Fentanyl infusion is equal to Fentanyl transdermal patch = 1:1

Example:

Mary has a Fentanyl infusion at 25mcg/hr. You want to change her to a Fentanyl Patch. Her patch would be 25mcg/hr. – change patch every 72 hours.

** Note: The standard is to change fentanyl patches every 72 hours.**

Methadone

Methadone is an opioid that is used to relieve severe pain in patients who cannot be treated with other opioids. It is used for ATC treatment for chronic pain or to prevent withdrawal. Methadone can also be used when the patient has an allergy to morphine, has renal impairment, opioid-induced hallucinations, or intractable pain issues. It can be given to patients with g-tubes easily because it comes in liquid form or can be crushed and dissolved in water. Methadone has also been found to be less constipating than other opioids. Another advantage is that Methadone is less expensive than other opioids. Disadvantages of methadone include QT prolongation risk and a very long half-life of 8-59 hours. Other disadvantages can include the fact that methadone has numerous drug interactions, is unpredictable, and does not have a linear conversion. The higher the dose, the wider the equivalency ratio for potency.

24-hour total dose of oral Morphine	Conversion ratio (Oral Morphine: oral methadone)
< 30	2:1
30 – 99	4:1
100 – 299	8:1
300 – 499	12:1
500 – 999	15:1
>1000	20:1 or Greater

Helpful tips about Methadone

> ➢ **Methadone** Can cause QT prolongation.

> ➢ Methadone is excreted via the bowel in stool.

> ➢ **Methadone** Takes time to buildup in system. Long-half-life: up to 59 hours.

> ➢ **Methadone** Can be given PO, SC, IM, or IV.

> ➢ **Methadone** has a low street value due to the amount of time it takes to feel the full effects.

Practice Question #5

Mr. Smith is on Morphine ER 200 mg, two tablets twice a day and is being switched to methadone.

Step 1

Calculate the total daily oral morphine dosage. Two tablets of 200 mg each, taken twice daily is equal to 800 mg total oral morphine per day.

200 X 2 = 400 mg

400 X 2 = 800 mg

Step 2

Convert to methadone.

For a dosage of 800 mg per day, the conversion ratio of morphine to methadone is 15:1

800mg of oral morphine is equivalent to 1 mg Methadone

800 x 1 = 800

800 / 15 = 53 mg methadone per day

Step 3

Reduce the dosage by 50% for incomplete cross-tolerance.

53 mg X 0.50 = 26.5 mg methadone

Round to 27mg

Step 4

Methadone is started at three times per day.

27 / 3 = 9mg (TID) of methadone.

Methadone comes in 5mg and 10mg tablets.

Give 10 mg of methadone three times per day.

Step 5

Determine prn dose of morphine.

The prn dose should be 10% of the total daily opioid dosage. Mr. Smith was already on 800 mg per day of oral morphine. 800 mg oral morphine × 10% = 80 mg every 1 to 2 hours as needed.

Pearls
for
Passing

- Fentanyl does not come in PO form; only IV and patch.
- Hydrocodone (Vicodin), Oxycodone (Percocet), and Tramadol only come in PO form.
- MS Contin is just long-acting morphine. Contin stands for continuous.
- Morphine 60mg = 25mcg Fentanyl patch.
- When converting opioids, remember to reduce the new opioid by 25-50%, unless the pain is intractable, (should not worry too much about cross-tolerance reduction if pain is uncontrolled; it's more about controlling the patient's pain).
- Methadone has a very long half-life (approximately 60 hours) and must build up in the patient's tissues before feeling relief. That is why this drug has little street value and is a good choice for patients living in a homeless shelter; it is less likely to be stolen. Methadone also comes in liquid form, which is good for tube feeding.

Medication Knowledge: Practice Test 6

1. Short-acting PO oxycodone 30mg is equivalent to 30mg of long-acting PO morphine.

    A) No, short-acting PO oxycodone 30mg is equivalent to 45mg PO morphine ER.

    B) Yes, they are equivalent.

    C) No, short-acting PO oxycodone 30mg is equivalent to 60mg PO morphine ER.

    D) No, short-acting PO oxycodone 30mg is equivalent to 120mg PO morphine ER.

2. 10mg IV morphine is equivalent to 30mg short-acting morphine.

    A) True

    B) False

3. Morphine concentrate is the same as:

    A) Extended-release morphine

    B) Oxycontin

    C) MS Contin

    D) Roxanol

4. A patient is on Morphine 30mg PO Q12H and MSIR 15mg Q4 hours prn. He is being switched to PCA morphine. What is the calculated basal and bolus rate?

    A) 3mg/hr. basal rate and 1.5mg bolus every 10 minutes.

    B) 2.34/hr. basal rate and 1.2 bolus rate every 10 minutes.

    C) 2.2mg/hr. basal rate and 0.5mg bolus every 10 minutes.

    D) 1.56mg/hr. basal rate and 0.78 mg bolus every 10 minutes.

5. Mrs. Steele is on 20mg of Oxycodone every 8 hours. She is being switched to PCA morphine. What dose should she be started on, using a 25% reduction for incomplete cross-intolerance?

    A) 0.99mg/hr. basal rate and 0.50mg bolus every 10 minutes.

    B) 2.34/hr. basal rate and 1.2 Bolus rate every 10 minutes.

    C) 0.94mg/hr. basal rate and 0.47mg Bolus every 10 minutes.

    D) 1.56mg/hr. b/ asal rate and 0.78 mg Bolus every 10 minutes.

6. Mrs. Moore is taking 50mg of tramadol QID. She is being switched to hydrocodone QID for poorly controlled pain. What would be her starting dose? (No reduction due to uncontrolled pain).

    A) 8.25mg (closest dose form 7.5mg/300)

    B) 10mg PO QID (10/300)

    C) 7.5mg PO TID (7.5/300)

    D) 12.5mg PO QID (closest dose form 10/300)

7. Mrs. Farmer is currently taking 7.5mg PO hydromorphone (Dilaudid) QID. She is being switched to oral morphine PO BID. What is her new morphine dose with a 25% reduction for incomplete cross-tolerance?

    A) 45mg PO BID

    B) 90mg PO BID

    C) 120mg PO BID

    D) 60mg PO QID

8. Mrs. Taylor is on 10mg of Hydrocodone TID. She is being switched to oxycodone BID for poorly controlled pain. What is her new dosage? (No reduction for uncontrolled pain)

    A) 12mg BID

    B) 7.5mg BID

    C) 10mg BID

    D) 15mg QID

9. MS Contin can be crushed.

    A) True

    B) False

10. OxyContin is the same as Oxycodone.

    A) True

    B) False

11. Methadone can be given as a rescue drug and can therefore be given prn.

    A) True

    B) False

12. Mrs. Cary is on 60mg Tramadol PO TID. She is being changed to Oxycodone PO QID. What should her starting dose be? No reduction.

    A) Start 5mg Oxycodone PO QID.

    B) Start 10mg Oxycodone PO QID.

    C) Start 10.5mg Oxycodone PO QID.

    D) Start 11mg Oxycodone PO QID.

13. The rule of thumb for a fentanyl patch is 2:1 to morphine.

    A) True

    B) False

14. When setting up a PCA pump, the bolus rate should be half of the basal rate.

    A) True

    B) False

15. The recommendation for prn medications is 20% to 25% of the daily long-acting dose.

    A) True

    B) False

16. 10mg of IV morphine is the same as 40mg of oral morphine.

    A) True

    B) False

17. Fentanyl can be given orally.

    A) True

    B) False

18. Hydrocodone, oxycodone, and tramadol can be given IV.

    A) True

    B) False

19. 30mg of oral morphine is equivalent to 30mg of Hydrocodone.

    A) True

    B) False

20. 20 mg of Oxycodone is equivalent to 50mg of Hydrocodone.

   A) True

   B) False

21. Mrs. Reid is being switched from morphine PCA to Hydromorphone (Dilaudid) PCA. She is currently on a 2mg basal rate and a 1mg bolus every 10 minutes. What will her new basal and bolus rate be? (Include a 25% reduction for incomplete cross tolerance).

   A) 1.5mg/hr basal rate, 0.2mg bolus rate every 10 minutes.

   B) 0.9mg/hr basal rate, 0.45mg bolus rate every 10 minutes.

   C) 1mg/hr basal rate, 0.3mg bolus rate every 10 minutes.

   D) 2mg/hr basal rate, 0.8mg bolus rate every 10 minutes.

22. Mrs. Cline is on 100mg PO morphine every 8 hours and MSIR 30mg PO every 2 hours prn. She is being switched to PO hydromorphone QID. What should her new dosage be with a 25% reduction for incomplete cross tolerance?

   A) 10mg PO QID

   B) 15mg PO BID

   C) 31mg PO QID

   D) 10mg PO TID

23. Mr. Kay is on oxycodone 60mg PO TID. He is being switched to oral morphine TID. What is his new dosage? (Include 25% reduction for incomplete cross tolerance)

   A) Morphine 180mg PO TID

   B) Morphine 20mg PO TID

   C) Morphine 67.5mg PO TID

   D) Morphine 30mg PO BID

24. Mr. Carter is on 4mg of IV morphine every 6 hours. He is being switched to oral morphine QID. What is his new dosage with a 25% reduction for incomplete cross-tolerance?

    A) Morphine 9mg PO QID

    B) Morphine 20mg PO QID

    C) Morphine 10mg PO QID

    D) Morphine 15mg PO QID

25. Mrs. Caplinger is on 3mg IV of hydromorphone every 6 hours. She is being switched to oxycodone PO QID. What is her new dosage with a 25% reduction for incomplete cross tolerance?

    A) 60mg oxycodone PO QID

    B) 40mg oxycodone PO QID

    C) 20mg oxycodone PO QID

    D) 30mg oxycodone PO QID

Practice Test 6: Answers and Rationales

1. Short-acting PO oxycodone 30mg is equivalent to 30mg of long-acting PO morphine.

    A) No, short-acting PO oxycodone 30mg is equivalent to 45mg PO morphine ER.

2. 10mg IV morphine is equivalent to 30mg short-acting morphine.

    A) True

3. Morphine concentrate is the same as:

    D) Roxanol

4. A patient is on Morphine 30mg PO Q12H and MSIR 15mg Q4 hours prn. He is being switched to PCA Morphine. What is the calculated basal and bolus rate?

    D) 1.56mg/hr. Basal rate and 0.78 mg bolus every 10 minutes.

Feedback:
30mg Morphine PO   =   10mg IV Morphine
150 mg = TDD
150 X 10 = 1500
1500 / 30 = 50
50 X 0.75 = 37.5 (25% reduction)
37.5 / 24 = 1.56 mg Basal rate
1.56 / 2 = 0.78 Bolus rate every 10 minutes.

5. Mrs. Steele is on 20mg of Oxycodone every 8 hours. She is being switched to IV morphine. What dose should she be started on using a 25% reduction for incomplete cross-intolerance?

    C) 0.94mg/hr. Basal rate and 0.47mg Bolus every 10 minutes.

Feedback:
20mg oxycodone = 10mg IV morphine
60mg TDD = 20 X 3 = 60
60 X 10 = 600mg
600mg / 20 = 30mg
30 X 0.75 = 22.5 (25% reduction)
22.5 / 24 = 0.94 / hr. Basal rate
0.94 / 2 = 0.47 Bolus rate every 10 minutes

6. Mrs. Moore is taking 50mg of tramadol QID. She is being switched to hydrocodone BID for poorly controlled pain. What would be her starting dose? (No reduction due to uncontrolled pain)

D) 12.5mg PO QID

Feedback:
120mg Tramadol = 30mg Hydrocodone
200mg TDD
200mg X 30mg = 6000mg
6000mg / 120 = 50mg
50mg / 4 = 12.5mg QID

Hydrocodone does not come in this dosage form, but this gives you a good idea of what the closest dose form would be. (10/300)

7. Mrs. Farmer is currently taking 7.5mg PO hydromorphone (Dilaudid) QID. She is being switched to oral morphine PO BID. What is her new morphine dose with a 25% reduction for incomplete cross tolerance?

A) 45mg PO BID

Feedback:
7.5mg PO hydromorphone = 30mg PO morphine
30mg TDD
30mg X 30mg = 900mg
900mg / 7.5mg = 120mg
120 X 0.75 = 90mg
90mg / 2 = 45mg PO BID

8. Mrs. Taylor is on 10mg of Hydrocodone TID. She is being switched to oxycodone BID for poorly controlled pain. What is her new dosage? (No reduction for uncontrolled pain)

C) **10**mg BID

Feedback:
30mg PO Hydrocodone = 20mg PO Oxycodone
30mg TDD
30mg X 20mg = 600mg
600mg / 30mg = 20mg
20mg / 2 = 10mg BID

9. MS Contin can be crushed.

     B) False

Feedback:
"Contin" stands for continuous. Long-acting medications are time-released and cannot be crushed.

10. Oxycontin is the same as Oxycodone.

     A) True

Feedback:
OxyContin is a brand name for oxycodone.

11. Methadone can be given as a rescue drug and can therefore be given prn.

     B) False

Feedback:
Methadone has an unpredictable half-life: anywhere from 8 to 59 hours.

12. Mrs. Cary is on 60mg Tramadol PO TID. She is being changed to Oxycodone PO QID. What should her starting dose be? No reduction

     B) Start 10mg Oxycodone PO QID.

Feedback:
120mg Tramadol = 20mg Oxycodone
240 X 20 = 4800
4800 / 120 = 40
40 / 4 = 10mg

13. The rule of thumb for a fentanyl patch is 2:1 to morphine.

     A) True

Feedback:
2mg oral morphine to 1 mcg/hour fentanyl patch.

14. When setting up a PCA pump, the bolus rate should be half of the basal rate.

     A) True
Feedback:

The bolus rate is typically half of the basal rate, given every 10-15 mins on demand.
15. The recommendation for prn medications is 20% to 25% of the daily long-acting dose.

    B) False

Feedback:
The recommendation for prn medications is 10% to 15% of the daily long-acting dose.

16. 10mg of IV morphine is the same as 40mg of oral morphine.

    B) False

Feedback:
10mg of IV morphine is the same as 30mg of oral morphine.

17. Fentanyl can be given orally.

    B) False

Feedback:
Fentanyl can be given IV or by a transdermal patch.

18. Hydrocodone, oxycodone, and tramadol can be given IV.

    B) False

Feedback:
Hydrocodone, oxycodone, and tramadol are given orally.

19. 30mg of oral morphine is equivalent to 30mg of Hydrocodone.

    A) True

20. 20 mg of Oxycodone is equivalent to 50mg of Hydrocodone.

    B) False

Feedback:
20 mg of Oxycodone is equivalent to 30mg of Hydrocodone.

21. Mrs. Reid is being switched from morphine PCA to hydromorphone (Dilaudid) PCA. She is currently on a 2mg basal rate and a 1mg bolus every 10 minutes. What will her new basal and bolus rate be? (Include a 25% reduction for incomplete cross tolerance)

    B) 0.9mg/hr. Basal rate, 0.45mg bolus rate every 10 minutes.

Feedback:
Total 24-hour morphine dose is:
2mg / hr. X 24 = 48mg
1mg every 10 mins = 6mg / hr. 6 x 24 = 144mg
144 + 48 = 192mg daily morphine

10mg IV morphine = 1.5mg IV hydromorphone
192mg morphine TDD

192 X 1.5 = 288
288 / 10 = 28.8
28.8 X 0.75 = 21.6 (25% reduction)
21.6 / 24 = 0.9mg / hr. basal rate
0.9 / 2 = 0.45mg bolus rate every 10 minutes

22. Mrs. Cline is on 100mg PO morphine every 8 hours and MSIR 30mg PO every 2 hours prn. She is being switched to PO hydromorphone QID. What should her new dosage be with a 25% reduction for incomplete cross tolerance?

   C) 31mg PO QID

Feedback:
100mg X 3 = 300mg, 30mg X 12 = 360mg   300mg + 360mg = 660mg total morphine

30mg PO morphine   =   7.5mg PO hydromorphone
660mg TDD

660 X 7.5 = 4950
4950 / 30 = 165
Reduce by 25%
165 X 0.75 = 123.75
123.75 / 4 = 30.94 (round up)
31mg QID

23. Mr. Kay is on oxycodone 60mg PO TID. He is being switched to oral morphine TID. What is his new dosage? (Include 25% reduction for incomplete cross tolerance)

   C) Morphine 67.5mg PO TID

Feedback:
20mg PO oxycodone= 30mg PO morphine
180mg TDD (total daily dose)
180 X 30 = 5400
5400 / 20 = 270
270 X 0.75 = 202.5
202.5 / 3 = 67.5mg of oral morphine TID

24. Mr. Carter is on 4mg of IV morphine every 6 hours. He is being switched to oral morphine QID. What is his new dosage with a 25% reduction for incomplete cross-tolerance?

    A) Morphine 9mg PO QID

Feedback:
10mg IV morphine = 30mg PO morphine
16mg TDD
16 X 30 = 480
480 / 10 = 48
48 X 0.75 = 36
36 / 4 = 9mg PO QID

25. Mrs. Caplinger is on 3mg IV of hydromorphone every 6 hours. She is being switched to oxycodone PO QID. What is her new dosage with a 25% reduction for incomplete cross-tolerance?

    D) 30mg oxycodone PO QID

Feedback:
1.5mg IV hydromorphone = 20mg PO oxycodone
12mg TDD of hydromorphone
12 X 20 = 240
240 / 1.5 = 160
160 X 0.75 = 120 (25% reduction)
120 / 4 = 30mg oxycodone PO QID

Scales

Scales are heavily reflected on the certification examination. Objective, evidence-based data is important for quality, cost-effective care. Measurable data, such as scales, are also important because it is part of the Medicare guidelines for hospice eligibility. The following pages have the most frequently used scales, and it would greatly benefit test-takers to memorize the Medicare eligibility requirements for hospice regarding the following scales.

Functional Assessment Staging Tool (FAST): Used to assess disease

progression in Alzheimer's Disease.

1	No difficulty either subjectively or objectively.
2	Complains of forgetting location of objects. Subjective work difficulties.
3	Decreased job functioning evident to co-workers. Difficulty in traveling to new locations. Decreased organizational capacity.
4	Decreased ability to perform complex task, (ie; planning, handling finances).
5	Requires assistance in choosing proper clothing to wear for the day, season, or occasion.
6	Demonstrates any of the following with more frequency: A) Improperly putting on clothes, without assistance or cueing. B) Unable to bathe properly (ie; not able to choose water temperature). C) Inability to handle mechanics of toileting. (ie; forgetting to flush, does not wipe properly or dispose of toilet tissue). D) Urinary incontinence E) Fecal incontinence.
7	Ability to speak limited to: A) Speech ability is limited to approximately 6 words or less in an average day or in the course of an intensive interview. B) Speech ability is limited to a single intelligible word in and average day or the person my repeat the same word consistently. C) Ambulatory ability is lost (cannot walk without assistance). D) Cannot sit up without assistance (the pt. will fall over if there are not lateral arm rests on chair). E) Loss of ability to smile. F) Loss of ability to hold up head independently.

Edmonton Symptom Assessment Scale (ESAS):

Used in cancer patients.

No Pain	0 1 2 3 4 5 6 7 8 9 10	Worst possible Pain
No Tiredness (Tiredness = lack of energy)	0 1 2 3 4 5 6 7 8 9 10	Worst Possible Tiredness
No Drowsiness (Drowsiness = feeling sleepy)	0 1 2 3 4 5 6 7 8 9 10	Worst Possible Drowsiness
No Nausea	0 1 2 3 4 5 6 7 8 9 10	Worst Possible Nausea
No Lack of Appetite	0 1 2 3 4 5 6 7 8 9 10	Worst Possible Lack of Appetite
No Shortness of Breath	0 1 2 3 4 5 6 7 8 9 10	Worst Possible Shortness of Breath
No Depression (Depression = feeling sad)	0 1 2 3 4 5 6 7 8 9 10	Worst Possible Depression
No Anxiety (Anxiety = feeling nervous)	0 1 2 3 4 5 6 7 8 9 10	Worst Possible Anxiety
Best Wellbeing (Wellbeing = how you feel overall)	0 1 2 3 4 5 6 7 8 9 10	Worst Possible Wellbeing
No _____ (Other Problem)	0 1 2 3 4 5 6 7 8 9 10	Worst Possible --------------

Pain Assessment in Advanced Dementia (PAINAD) Scale

Items	Score = 0	Score = 1	Score = 2	Score
Breathing (Independent of vocalization)	Normal	*Occasional labored Breathing *Short periods of hyperventilation	*Noisy labored Breathing *long period of hyperventilation *Cheyne-stokes respirations	
Negative Vocalization	None	*Occasional moan or groan *Low level of speech with a negative or disapproving quality	*Repeated troubled calling out *Loud moaning or groaning *Crying	
Facial expression	Smiling or inexpressive	*Sad *Frightened *Frown	*Facial grimacing	
Body language	Relaxed	*Tense *Distressed pacing *Fidgeting	*Rigid *Fists clenched *Knees pulled up *Striking out	
Consolability	No need to Console	*Distracted or reassured by voice or touch	*Unable to console, distract, or reassure	
Total				

Palliative Performance Scale (PPS) — One of the most heavily used scales in hospice and palliative care. This is due to the amount of diseases with which it can be used and its relevance to Medicare standards when deciding if a patient is appropriate for hospice care.

%	Ambulation	Activity and Evidence of Disease	Self-Care	Intake	Level of Conscious
100	Full	Normal activity No evidence of disease	Full	Normal	Full
90	Full	Normal activity Some evidence of disease	Full	Normal	Full
80	Full	Normal activity With effort, some evidence of disease	Full	Normal or reduced	Full
70	Reduced	Unable to do normal work, some evidence of disease	Full	Normal or reduced	Full
60	Reduced	Unable to do hobby or some housework Significant disease	Occasional assistance necessary	Normal or reduced	Full or Confusion
50	Mainly Sit/lie	Unable to do any work, extensive disease	Considerable assistance required	Normal or reduced	Full or Confusion
40	Mainly Sit/lie	Unable to do any Work, extensive disease	Mainly assistance	Normal or reduced	Full, drowsy or confusion
30	Totally bed bound	Unable to do any Work, extensive disease	Total care	Reduced	Full, drowsy or confusion
20	Totally bed bound	Unable to do any Work, extensive disease	Total care	Minimal sips	Full, drowsy or confusion
10	Totally bed bound	Unable to do any Work, extensive disease	Total care	Mouth care only	Drowsy or coma
0	Death	Death	Death	Death	Death

Karnofsky Performance Status Scale – Predisposed the PPS scale

and used primarily for cancer patients.

Mild Able to carry on normal activity and to work; no special care needed.	100	Normal, no complaints, no evidence of disease
Mild Able to carry on normal activity and to work; no special care needed.	90	Able to carry on normal activity; minor signs or symptoms of disease
Mild Able to carry on normal activity and to work; no special care needed.	80	Normal activity with effort; some signs or symptoms of disease
Moderate Unable to work, able to live at home and care for most personal needs; varying amount of assistance needed.	70	Cares for self; unable to carry on normal activity or to do active work
Moderate Unable to work, able to live at home and care for most personal needs; varying amount of assistance needed.	60	Requires occasional assistance, but can care for most of their personal needs
Moderate Unable to work, able to live at home and care for most personal needs; varying amount of assistance needed.	50	Requires considerable assistance and frequent medical care
Severe Unable to care for self; requires equivalent of institutional or hospital care; disease may be progressing rapidly.	40	Disabled; requires special care and assistance
Severe Unable to care for self; requires equivalent of institutional or hospital care; disease may be progressing rapidly.	30	Severely disabled; hospital admissions is indicated although death is not imminent
Severe Unable to care for self; requires equivalent of institutional or hospital care; disease may be progressing rapidly.	20	Very sick; hospital admission necessary; active supportive treatment necessary
Severe Unable to care for self; requires equivalent of institutional or hospital care; disease may be progressing rapidly.	10	Moribund; fatal processes progressing rapidly
Death	0	**Dead**

Made in the USA
Columbia, SC
14 April 2024